# Your Palm—A Road Map to Life

For nearly 2,000 years, the art and science of palmistry has been shrouded in secrecy. Now you can gain immediate access to this hidden knowledge by reading *The Instant Palm Reader*.

You'll see how the road of life is mapped out in the palm of your hand—your character, personality, childhood, career, finances, family, love life, talents, happiness, and destiny. By following the illustrated guide you can perform your own personal palm reading, just like a pro!

*The Instant Palm Reader* shows you how your hands contain the blueprint of your body, mind, and spirit—your true and sacred self. Your characteristics, skills, and inherent talents are imprinted in your mind and transferred as images onto your palm. You hold the past, present, and future in the palm of your hand.

This book is the brainchild of former aerospace scientist Linda Domin. She has employed the same meticulous attention to detail that was demanded for the space shuttle program. By decoding all the palm line systems of the major schools of palmistry and integrating them with her own findings, she has created a palm reading system which has been applauded for its accuracy.

## About the Author

Linda Domin received her M.S. degree in zoology and botany from the Technical University of Darmstadt, West Germany, and has worked as a research scientist for Grumman Allied Corporation in the Hypobaric Food Storage Program. She has also worked as a high school and college biology instructor and as a horticultural consultant for the city of Miami. She currently lives in Miami, where she does private consultations in palm analysis.

## To Write to the Author

If you wish to contact the author or would like more information about this book, please write to the author in care of Llewellyn Worldwide, and we will forward your request. Both the author and publisher appreciate hearing from you and learning of your enjoyment of this book and how it has helped you. Llewellyn Worldwide cannot guarantee that every letter written to the author can be answered, but all will be forwarded. Please write to:

Linda Domin
c/o Llewellyn Worldwide
P.O. Box 64383, Dept. K232-1, St. Paul, MN 55164-0383, U.S.A.
Please enclose a self-addressed, stamped envelope for reply,
or $1.00 to cover costs.
If outside the U.S.A., enclose international postal reply coupon.

## About Llewellyn's New Age Series

The "New Age"—it's a phrase we use, but what does it mean? Does it mean the changing of the Zodiacal Tides, that we are entering the Aquarian Age? Does it mean that a new Messiah is coming to correct all that is wrong and make Earth into a Garden? Probably not—but the idea of a *major change* is there, combined with awareness that Earth *can be* a Garden; that war, crime, poverty, disease, etc., are not necessary "evils."

Optimists, dreamers, scientists . . . nearly all of us believe in a "better tomorrow," but that somehow we can do things now that will make for a better future life for ourselves and for coming generations.

In one sense, we all know "there's nothing new under the Heavens," and in another sense that "every day makes a new world." The difference is in our consciousness. And this is what the New Age is all about: it's a major change in consciousness found within each of us as we learn to bring forth and manifest "powers" that Humanity has always potentially had.

Evolution moves in "leaps." Individuals struggle to develop talents and powers, and their efforts build a "power bank" in the Collective Unconsciousness, the "soul" of Humanity that suddenly makes these same talents and powers easier access for the majority.

Those who talk about a New Age believe a new level of consciousness is becoming accessible that will allow anyone to manifest powers previously restricted to the few who had worked strenuously for them: powers such as Healing (for self and others), Creative Visualization, Psychic Perception, Out-of-Body Consciousness and more.

You still have to learn the rules for developing and applying these powers, but it is more like a "relearning" than a *new* learning, because with the New Age it is as if the basis for these had become genetic.

The books in the New Age series are as much about *Attitude and Awareness* as they are about the "mechanics" for learning and using Psychic, Mental, Spiritual, or Parapsychological Powers. Understanding that the Human Being is indeed a "potential god/goddess" is the first step toward the realization of that potential: expressing in outer life the inner creative powers.

# Instant
# Palm Reader

## A Road Map to Life

(Formerly titled *Palmascope*)

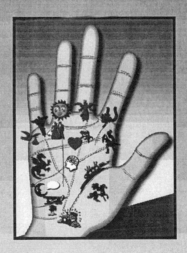

# Linda Domin

1997
Llewellyn Publications
St. Paul, Minnesota, U.S.A. 55164-0383

FIRST EDITION
First Printing, 1997
(formerly titled *Palmuscope*)

Cover Design: Anne Marie Garrison
Cover Illustration: RKB Studios
Interior Illustrations: Charles Smith

Library of Congress Cataloging-in-Publication Data
Domin, Linda, 1946–
    Instant Palm Reader.
    (Llewellyn's new age series)
    Bibliography: p.
    1. Palmistry.  I. Title.  II. Series.
BF921.D66    1997   133.6   88-29665
ISBN 1-56718-232-1

LLEWELLYN PUBLICATIONS
A Division of Llewellyn Worldwide, Ltd.
P.O. Box 64383, St. Paul MN 55164-0383

# DEDICATION

*This book is lovingly dedicated
to my mother, Gilda,
without whose support
this book would not have been possible.*

# Contents

## Introduction

Picture the palm of your hand as an aerial view of all the scenes you travel in the course of a lifetime. The curving and crossing lines map out the roads along which you travel. Your journey's beginning: Birth! Could the changing landscapes of life, your journey of experiences, actually be written on the palm of your hand? Soon you will find out.

Instant Palm Reader is a tested method, a step-by-step guided tour along the road of life, as mapped out in the lines on the palm of your hand. With it you can read a palm, like a professional, within minutes of picking up this book. Follow the pictorial guide to palm lines and assemble your own very personal and accurate palm analysis in an instant.

Your palm reading will explain the meaning of all your palm lines and the effect each line has upon numerous phases of your life (i.e., your character, personality, childhood, career, finances, family life, talents, love life, happiness, mission in life, needs, education, moods, and destiny). After a few minutes on your tour, you will be rewarded with psychologically uplifting and thrillingly hopeful new discoveries about yourself.

## Advantages of Instant Palm Reader

The palm reading tour you are about to make condenses the fruits and labors of thousands of years of palmistry into a few minutes of your time. Let's look back for a moment to see how and why this was done.

For centuries humankind has attributed mystical qualities to the lines on the palm of the hand. A fascination for this subject prompted palmists throughout history to record and define the meanings of these lines. People searching for answers relied heavily upon these meanings to help solve life's problems.

On what basis did the palmists of the past arrive at their conclusions? By comparing the hands of a great number of people, palmists found that similarities in character were visible as similarities in lines. If the palmist kept a record of his or her findings and his/her teachings had appeal, a school of palmistry was soon born around his/her reputation.

You might wonder why there are so many schools of palmistry; in fact, there are hundreds. Different schools take pride in their particular specialization. One school might specialize in reading only the major lines; another might stress minor lines; yet another might concentrate on the shape of the hand. Some focus on predictions about the future; others serve only to analyze personality and character. The newest schools interrelate with astrology and medical diagnostics.

The body of knowledge supporting palmistry is based on empirical evidence, recorded since the year 1500 B.C. Noted palmists always made an effort to hide or convolute their wealth of information, thereby weaving a web of mystery around their particular school. These schools operated like businesses, and secrecy protected them from competitors and laymen.

To make this book possible, ancient and modern manuscripts were collected from all the different schools around the globe. Their contents were assembled into a simple, easy-to-follow flip chart. To complete this feat, thousands of palm lines were translated, decoded, and catalogued in logical order. This new arrangement was specially designed to allow anyone to assemble their own personal palm reading accurately, without any prior knowledge of the subject, simply by following the pictures.

Your palm analysis is carefully designed to help you become more in touch with yourself and the world, and to help answer questions otherwise unanswerable by conventional means. Besides that, it is exciting, educational, and entertaining.

## History of Palmistry

For the past fifty centuries humankind has attributed a mystical quality to the lines in the palm of the hand. Palmistry records can be traced as far back as the Vedic Scriptures of the earliest Indian Cultures (1500 B.C.), when it was practiced by the Brahmins. In China, palmistry was popular as early as 3000 B.C. Much of this ancient art is preserved in China and Japan today and practiced in the strictest traditions of the past.

Among the ancient Romans, palmistry was a part of the official religion of state and was regularly used in parlimentary procedure. Aristotle, "the Father of Natural Science and Philosophy," presented a palmistry treatise to Alexander the Great, it is said, in letters of gold. Early Greek contributors were the physicians Galen, founder of experimental physiology, and Hippocrates, "Father of Medicine."

In 400 B.C. a treatise on palmistry reappeared in England dedicated to Belin, the twenty-third King of the Britons. It wasn't until the Middle Ages when scholars such as Johann von Hagen and Paracelsus (the genius of science and medicine) revived and systematized palmistry. It was then believed that the heavenly bodies Mars, Venus, Jupiter, Saturn, Apollo, Mercury, and the Moon governed the patterns of the different palm lines found in the hand, and that a person could read his or her God-directed mission in life in the configuration of lines mapped out in his/her palm.

Throughout the Middle Ages palm reading flourished in all the major European cities, where it was received with unanimous recognition as a respected school of thought at all universities. A German physician, Rothman, discarded many unsubstantial beliefs and superstitions about palmistry and introduced a uniform system of hand reading, which was adapted into the medical school curricula.

In the nineteenth century D'Arpentigny, a French scholar, modernized palmistry through a lifetime of scientific studies devoted to the charting of hundreds of thousands of palm lines with their corresponding characteristics. Another important figure in the modernization of palmistry was Desbarrolles, who in 1879 invented a palm-printing technique that enabled him to study and discover the constantly changing, appearing and disappearing lines on the same palm.

The twentieth century brought with it humankind's dependence upon newly discovered technologies and the readiness to relinquish the sacred traditions of the past. The "new" was purported to be better than the "old," and with this new philosophy, palmistry was reduced to the level of a parlor game.

Scientists might scoff at palmistry, but no scientist to date has come up with a study to invalidate it. Surprisingly, many scientists stand in its defense. Dr. Charlotte Wolff, Polish-born and English-educated physician and psychologist, is the modern harbinger of scientific palmistry (1940). In her twenty years of intense research she accomplished the remarkable feat of classifying over 90,000 hands according to human character types, psychological profiles, and physical and mental anomalies. She swept through the then-unexplored field of psychology with innovative genius and aided palmistry in winning credibility in the scientific community.

Today there is a whole science, dermatoglyphics, built around genetic factors influencing the finger ridges as well as the contour of the palm lines, along with their clinical significances. Contributors of the past two decades are Dr. S.B. Holt, Dr. M.S. Elbualy, and Dr. J.D. Schindler.

Dr. Theodore J. Berry, in his book "The Hand as a Mirror of Systematic Diseases," reminds us of a variety of serious diseases that can be detected by the study of a patient's hands. Included are German measles, mitric heart valve prolapse, mongolism, Turner's syndrome, and dystrophy.

Anatomists explain the appearance of the lines in the palm of the hand as flexural creases caused by opening and closing of the hand. They, however, cannot explain the fact that newborn infants oftentimes have more lines on their palms than adults.

As palmistry reemerges in the Western world to regain repute, many other parts of the world, which have never stopped practicing palmistry seriously, continue to go about it as they did thousands of years ago. Chinese cities are dotted with palmistry practices. Consulting a palmist before making major decisions has been a practice in China for over 2,000 years. In Japan major magazines and newspapers carry daily palmistry columns, just as ours carry horoscopes. Many children in the Far East are taken to the palmist before they are baptized. The following in South America is so great that newsstands carry popular-selling magazines totally devoted to palmistry.

In these countries palmistry is trusted to give people the answers that religion, medicine, business, and scholars can't.

## The Theory Behind Palmistry and How it Works

We all judge people by the lines and character of their faces, that is, by their "physiognomy." Therefore it is not surpising that for thousands of years it has also been a popular belief that palmistry describes the different personality and character traits inscribed upon the lines of the palm. Even the human body as a whole has been classified by anthropologists and sociologists into the different character and personality types of the ectosomes, leptosomes, and mesosomes.

Aristotle was the first to maintain that the grooves, creases, and lines in the palm are a result of nervous and muscular interplay directed by the brain. In light of modern anatomy, the hand can be viewed as an endpoint of nerve impulses coming from the brain. Every thousandth of a second (millisecond), countless nerve impulses coming from the brain connect with muscles in the hand, causing the muscles of the hand to be in constant flection—a kind of micro-movement that is so small, it is invisible to the naked eye.

Palmist Judith Hipskind considers this constant motion to be the direct cause of lines and creases. She feels that it is this indirect channeling of the expression of a person's feelings, wants, needs, actions, and unconscious mind (all registered and stored in the brain) that makes up the substance of palmistry. This implies that the palm lines may be directly influenced by a part of the mind that knows more about us and our direction in life than we care or are able to admit.

There is an evolutionary correlation between the hand and the brain. It is a fact that a large percentage of nerve fibers leading from the brain are projected towards the outer extremities and terminate in a ray pattern in the hands and in the feet. This strengthens the conclusion that the hand and the foot (the Chinese still practice the art of the feet, called *podology*) developed *pari passu* with the brain, which is the seat of the mind. Information stored in the brain is then projected upon the surface of the palm, like a video camera projects an image through a network of cables onto a screen.

Some palmists, particularly William Benham, feel strongly that the Will and the Divine Mind cooperate in etching lines that bear significance of destiny onto the palm.

Thoughts harbored over a long period of time do become attitudes and eventually are molded into a person's personality. Hipskind suggests that thoughts activated in the brain transmit responses that end in the hands; these impulses eventually become registered in the palm as fine lines, and later as stronger lines. Since a person's personality undergoes continuous change, Hipskind concludes that the palm print undergoes a distinct transformation every few years to accommodate a person's changing personality, outlook, and experiences. You might wish to read your own palm again after a time to explore the changes in yourself.

Other noted contemporary palmists, such as Fred Gettings, Mir Bashir, and Marcel Broekman, have built their reputation around extensive files of palm prints from the same individuals that have been collected and compared over the years. They unanimously attest that lines come (and also go) with time.

It is a fascinating and engaging pastime to keep a record of your own palm print, while doing an introspective study of your life. The famed psychiatrist C.G. Jung believed that palmistry had the potential of unlocking secrets hidden deeply within the subconscious. He used palmistry frequently in his psychiatric practice to evaluate patients and took advantage of palmistry's intuitive potential by anticipating future problems of his patients. C.G. Jung is quoted as having said, "Hands, whose shape and functioning are so intimately connected with the psyche, might provide revealing and therefore interpretable expressions of psychical peculiarity of the human character."

Psychos, author of the standard work *The Complete Guide to Palmistry*, contends that the hand is the servant of the brain, and as such reflects the kind of brain behind it.

The trained palmist can detect lines in the palm that reveal a person's basic character and personality; changes in his or her environment; a person's concealed emotional world with all its yearnings, talents, ambitions, conflicts, dreams; and abilities from before birth until after death.

Your hands contain the physical, emotional, and mental picture of the real you. The characteristics, skills, and abilities as they are imprinted upon your hands are intended as guidelines for a happier and more fulfilling life, not as dreadful

5

forecasts of impending evil. And palmistry is meant to be used as a stepping-stone on the way to personal improvement and enlightenment.

## The Geography of the Lines on the Palm

In the same way that a global relief map of the earth illustrates the shape of our planet with its mountains, valleys, rivers, rivulets, and open plains, so does the palm of your hand with its mounts, lines, and configurations represent the picture of your life.

The lines come in all shapes and sizes: deep or shallow, branched or tasseled, long or short, winding or crosshatched . . . palmistry utilizes every facet of detail of thousands of lines. And the lines gain their true significance based upon where they are located on the palm, where they begin and end, what areas they transect, and what areas they connect.

All palms contain six basic lines in common. These are called *major* lines and are named from top to bottom: the *Heart Line*, the *Head Line*, and the *Life Line*. Looking down at your right hand, they are named from left to right: the *Mercury Line*, the *Apollo Line*, and the *Saturn Line*.

Each line with its own special nomenclature and design depicts a certain course of action in a person's life which can be summed up as follows:

**Heart Line:** deals with the emotions, a person's loving nature, insecurities, marriages, dependence and independence

**Head Line:** indicative of career, intellect, reasoning powers, career attitudes, potentials for success

**Life Line:** is not the indicator of length of life— rather it relates to the pattern and quality of life, to physical vitality, to stability or imbalance, will power and logic

**Mercury Line:** relates to matters of health (in particular the nervous system) and to business and adventure and the spirit of discovery

**Apollo Line:** tells about utilization of creative energies and potentials for success through development of talents

**Saturn Line:** the important psychological revealer of strengths of character, career, friendships, life's daily problems, and general ability to succeed

Palms also have numerous other *minor lines*, which have self-explanatory names such as *Marriage Line, Line of Influence, Girdle of Venus* (denoting emotionalism, sexuality, and temperament), and *Ring of Solomon* (encompassing wisdom and psychic powers).

## The Configurations

Palms also have figurative markings called *configurations*, which are named for the shape they graphically represent, and they add to the meaning of the lines or areas they are near:

**Chains:** obscure goals, inclinations to deviate

**Tassels and Grilles:** setting of obstacles, struggles, and diminished abilities

**Breaks in Lines:** suggest weaknesses

**Branches:** give extra strength

**Islands:** indicate delays, injuries, and problems

**Crosses:** signify upheavals, violence, struggles, and blunders

**Quadrangles:** exaggerate or lessen a personality trait, depending upon size

**Triangles:** are known to improve luck or cause delays through crankiness

**Circles:** amplify physical or emotional health problems, or special talents and abilities

**Bars:** signify temporary impediments

**Stars:** accentuate strengths, and are associated with luckiness

**Squares:** strengthen the quality of any weak area

## The Fingers and Mounts

The fingers of the hand are also assigned names. They refer to the planets that govern the territory they represent. The thumb is named *Venus*, the index finger is assigned *Jupiter*, the middle finger is called *Saturn*, the ring finger *Apollo*, and the pinkie

*Mercury.*

The palm is divided into sectors of fleshy cushions called *mounts.* Under every finger there is a flesh cushion or mount, and these mounts carry the same name as the finger they are under. The mounts form a clockwise pattern, and going around the right hand starting under the little finger, they read: Mercury, Apollo, Saturn, Jupiter, Lower Mars, Venus, Moon, and Upper Mars.

You are probably asking here, "What does each planet mean?" Each planet stands for character and personality traits as below:

**Mercury:** buoyancy, wit, spirit, shrewdness

**Apollo:** compassion, love of beauty, artistic abilities, ability to be a success

**Saturn:** seriousness, cautiousness, gloom, superstition

**Jupiter:** leadership, honor, ambition, religiousness

**Lower Mars:** moral courage, self-control

**Venus:** benevolence, affection, humility, passion

**Moon:** sentimentality, imagination, self-centeredness

**Upper Mars:** resistance, coolness of spirit, calmness, and courage

The slightest deviation in the form of a line is important to a palmist. For example, a Life Line ideally surrounds the Mount of Venus, and one person in 500 will have such a perfectly formed line. More than likely, a Life Line will be anything but perfect; it will be wiry, branched, wiggly, even very short, or maybe broad and tasseled, and may be accompanied by any number of circles, dots, stars, squares, or crossing lines. These deviations are not egregiously unfortunate and negative, but serve the palmist as distinct clues to the many facets of one's life, personality, and character.

## Instructions for Reading Your Palm

The Self-Guided Tour Index is designed so that as you move along with your palm reading, you quickly become familiar with the strange names used in palmistry. And within a few moments you will be able to recognize the presence or absence of the different line designs in your own hand when compared to the index.

Start by just looking at your opened right palm, while turning the pages with your left hand and comparing your own palm lines with those pictured in the index. Left-handed people usually read their left palm.

Reference charts at the end of the index provide you with an overall view. Arrows and dotted circles and lines are only visual aids for your spatial orientation.

For those wishing to learn more about how palmistry works, there are additional chapters, including a short course for future professionals.

## The Self-Guided Tour Index

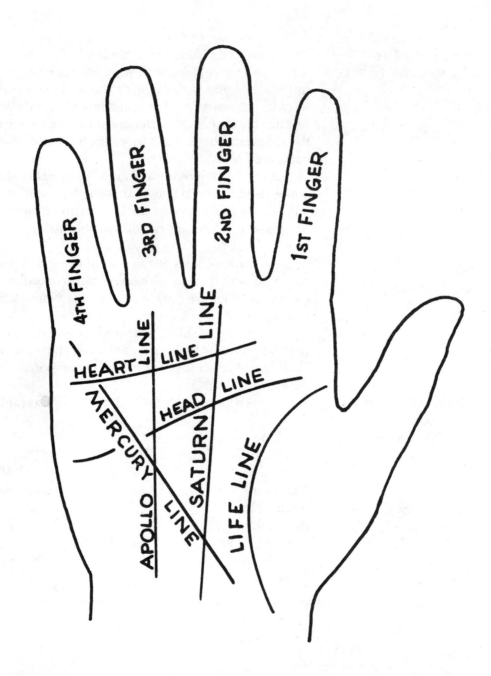

**MAIN LINES**

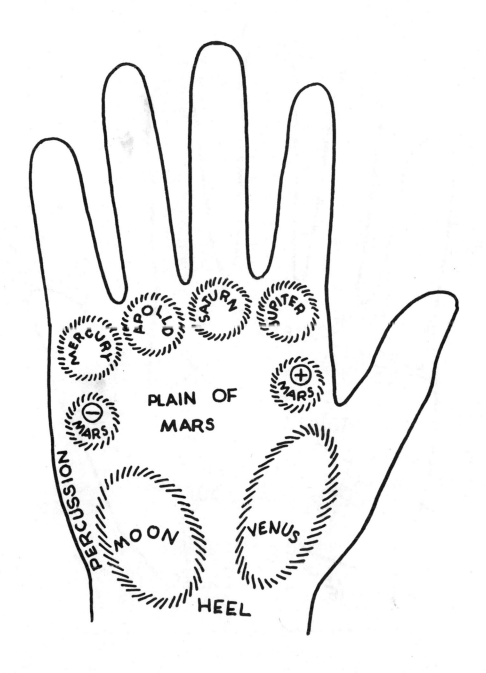

**MOUNTS**

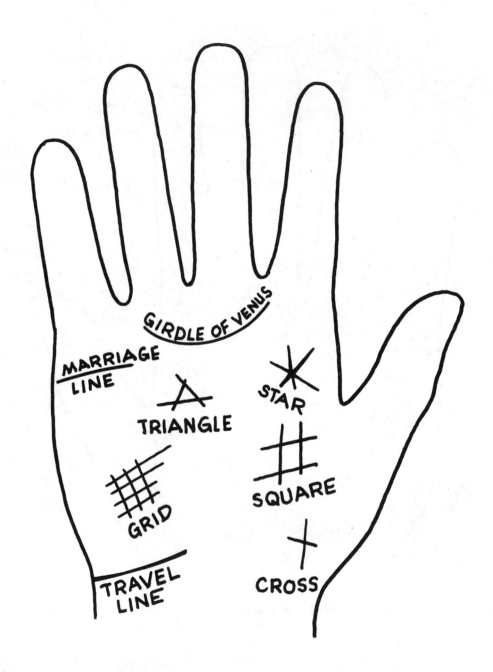

MARKS

# The Self-Guided Tour Index

# LIFE LINE

### -1-
### Your Life Line is thick and deeply etched.

You have a robust constitution. You are given by fate heavier loads to bear than most, because you possess powerful inner reserves. Others envy the way you throw off worry and emit an air of self-confidence. Although you are capable of great physical exertion, your phlegmatic habits dominate.

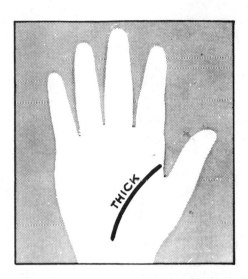

### -2-
### Your Life Line is thin.

You hide from others and avoid exposure to the world outside, locked inside your shell of protection. Within this shell you are safe from overexcitement, overwork, and all the unexpected things in life. Herein you carefully guard your energy levels in fear of burning out too soon, hoping to thus live a healthier and more creative life.

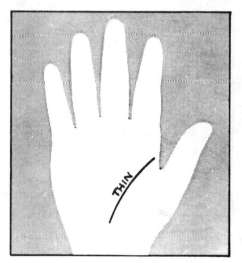

### -3-
### Your Life Line is faintly visible.

The faintness means you haven't even begun to taste of life yet. Unknowingly you deny yourself many of the pleasures of life, either because you consider them sinful or because they arouse deeper feelings of guilt. You can strengthen this line by participating in the world more and by accepting and making invitations. The greater your involvement in life, the bolder your line will become.

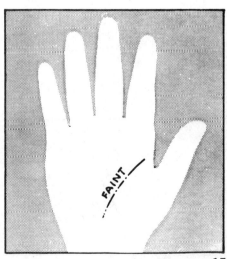

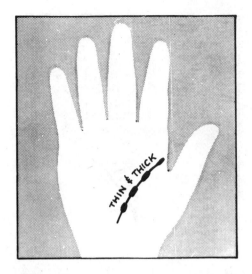

### -4-
### Your Life Line is unequal in thickness, thinner or hollower in some parts than in others.

Let out those strongly imprisoned emotions, and say NO to those who put you down. Stop letting others take advantage of you, even your friends. Your pent-up energies cause you to have a violent temper. When excited, you have ways of toning yourself down, bottling up your feelings, coddling your hatred, which has spoiled your ability to enjoy life.

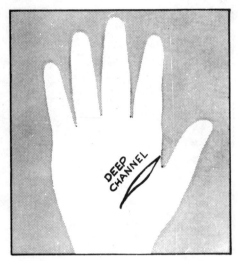

### -5-
### You have a short Life Line, which carves a deep channel.

You have the power to carefully control your mind and feelings, much more than most people. You show pride in the dominion over your actions and lead a life filled with purpose and determination. You have the habit of having the LAST WORD, and rebel when proven wrong. Your rebel nature is the limiting factor in your ascent to success.

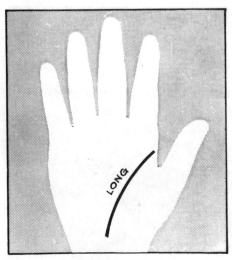

### -6-
### Your Life Line is long.

It has been decreed by a higher order that you live a long and healthy life. However, it is up to you through the proper use of your energies and talents to find fulfillment. Keep in mind this sign is not a free ticket to happiness and eternity, and that you must still continuously nourish and exercise your mind and your body.

### -7-
### Your Life Line has a ladder-like formation.

Your feelings are easily vexed by pushy, tactless persons, and once distracted you find it hard to get back in sync. Recuperate by placing yourself in soothing surroundings using the color blue. You are searching for a true friend to connect with, but suffer countless disappointments. You have very stringent requirements for a friendship.

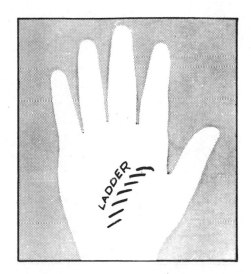

### -8-
### Your Life Line hugs the thumb closely.

You suddenly dismiss loved ones upon the slightest provocation, hurting yourself more than you hurt them. You avoid a sexual connotation in the way you dress and move, unconsciously avoiding intimacy. You underrate your attractiveness and are often oblivious to the feelings of others. A business partnership related to the arts could bring in a handsome profit for you.

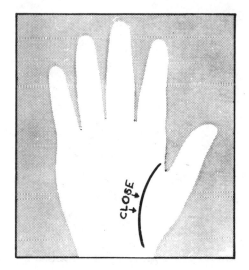

### -9-
### Your Life Line rises low on the palm around the Mount of Mars.

Unmasked sexual and romantic attractions are the forces that direct your life. You have been advised to practice more control over your emotions. You have put your whole heart into relationships that were thinly knit together purely through sexual magnetism. Through this your career drive might weaken. You have an endless reservoir of animal energies, and if some of them were siphoned off into your career, you could make remarkable headway.

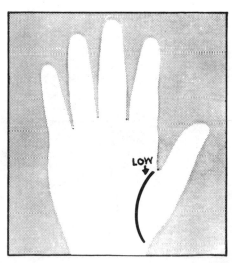

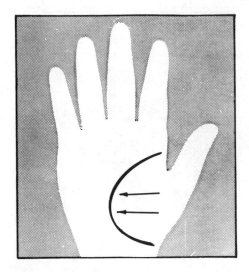

### -10-
### Your Life Line sweeps wide onto the palm.

Your ardent, enthusiastic character has the power to move others towards you. You show understanding for the underling. You take hardships upon yourself to relieve others. You must continuously replenish your spirits to keep up your enthusiasm. You try to be the leader in all relationships, even personal ones. Conflict over business ideas with mate pervade, but do not impair, your productivity.

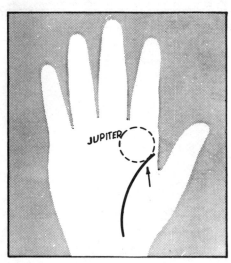

### -11-
### Your Life Line rises under the Mount of Jupiter.

A sure sign that you have control over your feelings and actions. Others confidently let you guide them through their difficult times. Your ambition to surmount troubles and win keeps you going long after others have given up. This drive coupled with your self-control wins you great honors.

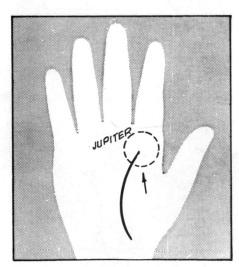

### -12-
### Your Life Line starts directly on the Mount of Jupiter.

You draw your energy from a dream of rising to great heights. Your far-reaching dream comes true not only because you have supercharged ambition, but also because of your congenial personality. You do not need to feign affections to gain social and financial status. You crave expansion and are addicted to success.

### -13-
### Your Life Line starts at a point high above the Mount of Jupiter.

No one is able to stop you once you have your mind set, whether it is set on success or bent on destruction. You have risen high above past competitors and are still not satisfied. You have a powerful drive for expansion and progress that will not tolerate running idle. Overcoming initial inertia seems to be a problem. But once your decision is firm, you go right to the finish line.

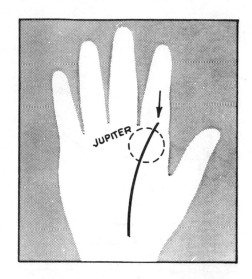

### -14-
### Your Life Line ends pointing towards the Mount of the Moon.

Your moods shift easily. Your disposition is like that of a restless drifter. From within comes an unexplainable compulsion to move farther and farther from familiar territory. The road feels like your second home. If continued, your feelings of patriotism for your country weaken and your destiny could be fulfilled in a distant land.

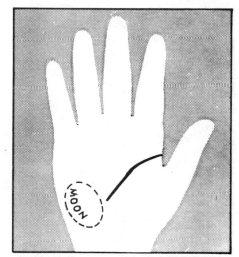

### -15-
### Your Life Line leaves its course and swerves to cover the Mount of the Moon.

Have you stopped to ask yourself the question, "Why am I running to and fro?" This line foreshadows an intensely restless drive. No matter what you are, you experience an uncomfortable urge to be somewhere else. You find it difficult to take charge of these runaway feelings. Your race with time has its origins in an unresolved inner turmoil. A remedy for this is to practice taking life at a snail's pace.

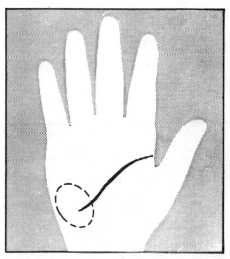

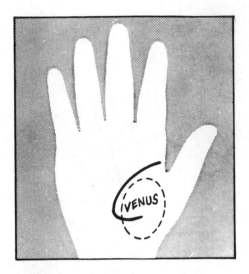

### -16-
### Your Life Line terminates in a direction pointing towards Venus.

Curiosity and wonderment about peoples of different cultures is a driving force. Wherever your curiosity and need to impress others leads you, ultimately you come home to roost. A mental bond exists between you and the home of your childhood. You seek to relive the mysterious past. Although you will travel about to fulfill desires, it can be considered a paradox that you only feel comfortable and relaxed in your own home.

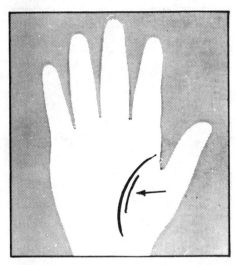

### -17-
### A thin line inside your Life Line reinforces it.

This line of reinforcement betokens a secret love. You are prone to love illicitly, and endure the pressures of concealment. You crave the excitement of the secret meetings. Your sense of reason is overpowered by your attraction to the opposite sex. This magnetism can zoom out of control and lead to actions that fill you with guilt. If you learn to accept this idiosyncrasy, you can make up for your failings towards others in different ways.

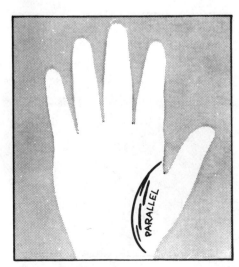

### -18-
### Inside your Life Line are a few lines that are finely etched in parallel arrangement.

You are an emotional and passionate person charged with love and quick with the tears. Caution is advised when your fiery passions swing into fixed hatred. An unrelenting search for revenge could drain you of your creative powers. This preoccupation can leave you powerless to solve the simpler of life's problems. Curbing flare-ups and sexual impulses will turn you into a powerhouse.

### -19-
### Many fine lines travel inside and parallel to your Life Line.

You are unable to live happily unless you receive a constant stream of love and attention from many sources at once. Several affairs, some of them simultaneous, are indicated. You are intensely emotional and passionate, and feel unsafe without your "ace in the hole." It would take a long wrangle with a very persistent suitor for you to settle down.

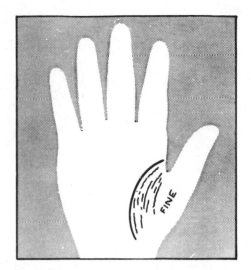

### -20-
### Concentric lines reinforce your Mounts of Venus and Mars.

Each curved line symbolizes a person of the opposite sex who exerts power over you. Their belief systems are imposed upon you, and you don't put up much of a fight in structuring and defending your own beliefs. One day the web underlying your thoughts might just become a reflection of others. Keep up your guard and emphasize your own philosophies.

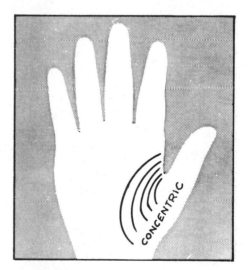

### -21-
### A line at the base of the Mount of Venus, which runs parallel to the Life Line, rises to the lower Mount of Mars.

Persons in whom you are greatly interested drift away from you, despite your attentiveness. You can even be at your best behavior—unintruding, careful, etc.—and still they will stray from you. You try to win people back and feel inadequate in doing so. The table will turn once you have some strong personal successes behind you.

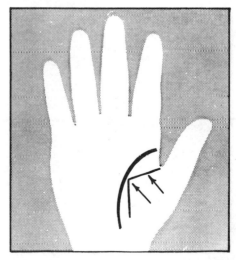

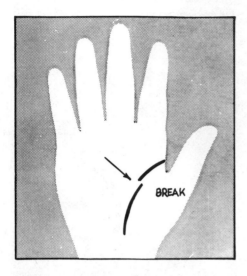

### -22-
### Your Life Line has a break in it.

You have allowed the memory of disagreeable times to etch its way deep into your body and soul. Admittedly, you have endured prolonged exposure to unpleasant conditions. There is a twofold absence of color in your life: Your daily surroundings are cheerless and, secondly, you feel that the excitement of life has slipped away. An entirely new lifestyle and outlook on life are in order.

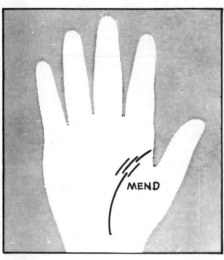

### -23-
### Your broken Life Line is mended by sister lines.

Say good-by to hard times and the dead ends that have been creeping up everywhere. Your road to happiness has been unblocked. The sister lines announce an alleviation of suffering. This mending process works in such a way that for every unpleasantness of the past, good fortune appears until good and evil are balanced. You must learn to grab opportunities without any hesitation as the wheel of fortune turns, no matter how brief they may be, and your luck will change.

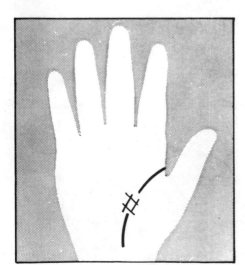

### -24-
### A gap in your Life Line is filled by a square.

Danger to your safety will be averted from time to time through the protective influence of the square. Others try hard behind the scenes to make you happy. You are able to endure much pain and spring back unscathed. The square is a protection from physical danger and helps restore you to full health after an accident or sickness.

### -25-
### A triangle is at the end of your Life Line.

You are a true diplomat, using every chance to turn problem-solving into a science. Your skill at settling differences is uncontested and one day could get you media attention. Friends stick to you because you help fortify their self-esteem. Even strangers turn to you for help, sensing this gift in you.

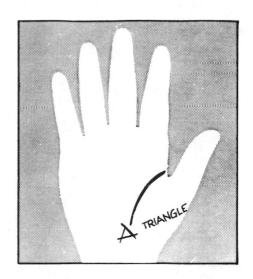

### -26-
### A tassel formation marks the end of your Life Line.

You scatter your mental efforts far and wide on projects that are doomed from the start. Although you work as hard as, if not harder than, others, you see little accomplishment. Ultimate failures will force you to concentrate all your efforts in one direction only, one project at a time. Distraction is your greatest foe. Look straight ahead—not left, not right.

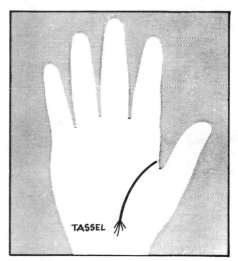

### -27-
### A small fork is at the base of your Life Line.

This is a common mark among people who are fond of reading, writing, sitting, and imagining. Vitality might be weakened with progressing age due to lack of regular, strenuous physical activity. You would love to experience the adventures of your dreams, but do not dare. If you were able to prove to yourself just once that you weren't afraid to face adventure, it could mean the beginning of a whole new life for you.

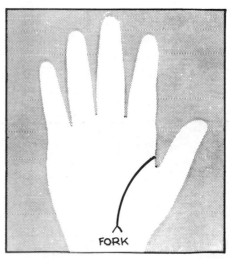

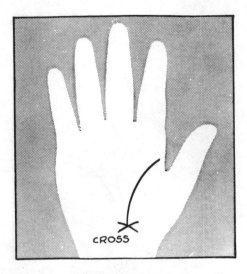

### -28-
### A cross is at the end of your Life Line.

This represents a kindhearted and capable, energetic individual. There are many facts behind the scenes that have been intentionally concealed from you. You never know the whole truth. You work best by yourself. Your life is an open book. Sometimes you need to be secretive to hold some rank and power over others. It is time for you to stop forgiving and start ignoring those who offend you.

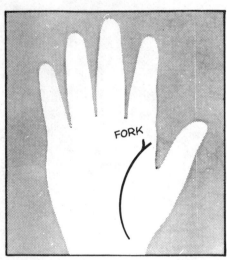

### -29-
### Your Life Line begins with a small fork under your first finger.

Every year of your profession has been marked by a progression. Sometimes you feel you are moving along with rockets at your heels. Since the time of your birth, your movement forward is pointed in the direction of that kind of success that benefits humankind. Engraved in your mind since childhood has been a great longing to be a star in your field.

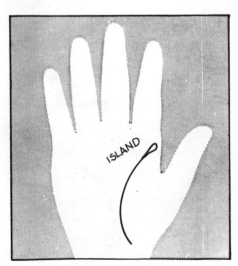

### -30-
### Your Life Line begins with an island formation.

A mystery of long ago has not been revealed to you. Many close to you know of it, but withhold secrets that occurred near or at the time of your birth. They wish to spare upsets. You have been harboring an instinct that there was more to be known. You might not solve this case, but it is worth a try, because it will offer an explanation for an inherent weakness.

### -31-
### Your Life Line is patterned in a chain fashion.

Your whole physical makeup is put together very delicately. The slightest painful experience can set you off balance. You are a keenly sensitive, impressionable, and creative person. Crude behavior repels you. As a child you were shocked by the crudeness of some adults. This is responsible for the ethical slant in your life. You look back at your childhood as a painful experience.

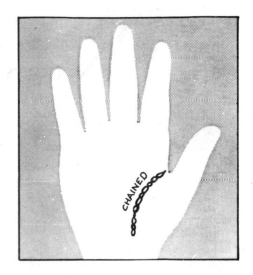

### -32-
### Your Life Line is shaped like a chain under the Mount of Jupiter.

Your physical constitution is fragile and easily affected by your environment. Even the slightest painful experience can set you off balance for a time. As a keenly impressionable child you were often repelled by the crude behavior of some adults. These memories have compelled you to impose a rigid set of ethics on others.

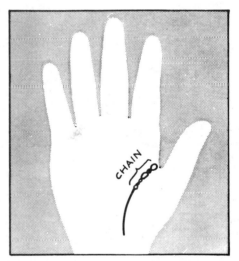

### -33-
### Your Life Line terminates abruptly with a few short parallel lines at the end.

The loss of vitality you perceive is not imagined. The past few years of life have been insipid and joyless. You are saddened by not having been able to reach goals and reap benefits wished for. You sense there is an invisible wall between you and opportunity. You are tired of being an observer. The parallel lines at the end herald a loosening of this posture, a breaking of the vicious cycle.

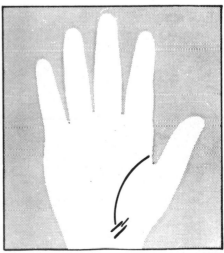

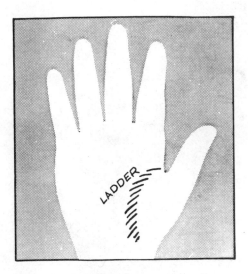

**-34-**
**Your Life Line is formed of many small lines arranged like closely set rungs of a ladder.**

You have been aspiring to improve upon many facets of your health and appearance for a long time now, and things just don't change for you. Pity from others angers you, and you will go to great lengths to conceal your misfortunes. You have focused for a long time on your shortcomings and have magnified them way out of proportion.

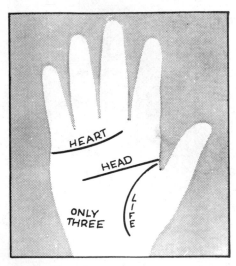

**-35-**
**You have a long, fine Heart Line, Life Line, and Head Line, and are without a trace of any Fate, Apollo, or Mercury Lines.**

As a child you had rather splendid expectations of what you would do when you grew up, and now you are disappointed about the outcome of things. You expected by now to look back at more significant accomplishments, and you are especially discouraged about your cash situation. Your patience will be rewarded, because for you things tend to arrive more slowly than for others.

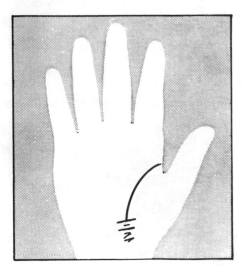

**-36-**
**Your Life Line terminates in a series of crossed lines.**

Your friends will say of you that you are an agreeable, good-natured, and good-humored pal. You have helped many in distress with your hospitality. You are accommodating to the wishes of others, sometimes to the point of self-sacrifice. Many of your great skills and aptitudes lie dormant because you do not have the courage to develop them.

### -37-
**A number of capillary lines gradually appear and gain strength at the end of your Life Line.**

Any premonitions you have had about an early or untimely death are unwarranted. The capillary lines annul bad omens. You need no longer feel troubled about impending disasters. These capillary lines reinforce you, making you able to bear the brunt of all forces directed against you.

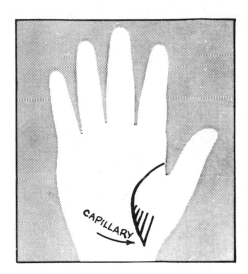

### -38-
**Upward branches on your Life Line are cut crosswise by Lines of Influence.**

In your lifetime you will be involved in various technical and legal proceedings against you. At times you will have to seriously defend your rights and fight against great odds. A forced departure from those you dearly love is a recurring phenomenon, and newly found loved ones quickly slip into their familiar places.

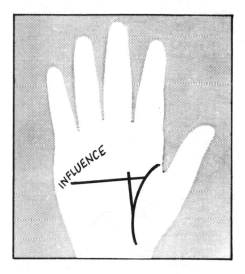

### -39-
**Your Life Line has a double formation, with the outer branch descending in a wide arch from Mars down to the Rascette.**

You are tired of being in charge of so much responsibility. You would like to take a permanent vacation from it all and partake in a simple life. Troubles bubble from out of nowhere faster than you can handle them. Many of these problems only dissolve through joint efforts. So don't waste your time struggling alone.

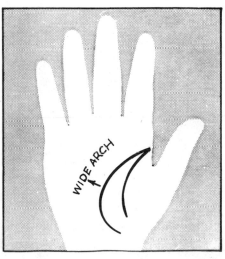

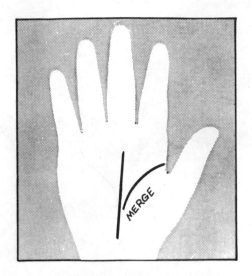

### -40-
### A broken end of your Life Line merges into your Line of Fate.

There is an unpredictable force in your life that appears and shapes the outcome of mishaps in your favor, no matter how dim the prospects seem at first. Your rescues from disaster always come just in the nick of time. One day these rescues will end, so prepare now to fend for yourself.

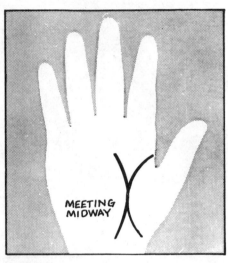

### -41-
### Your Life Line and Fate Line meet at a point in mid-course.

You have let your family influence major decisions. This has lessened your control over your life and diminished your chances for full realization of your potential. You must learn to trust your feelings, as you know yourself better than anyone else does. The second half of your life will be a reflection of the first half, mistakes and all, if you do not utilize the sleeping power within you to exert control over your decisions.

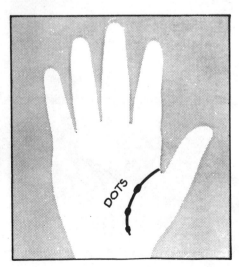

### -42-
### There are dot-like structures on your Life Line.

You are unhappy about what has happened to you in life—things that have been beyond your control. You want more fulfillment out of life, but are hindered by obstacles. There is no way around them, and you must plunge doggedly through them, one by one, and if you persist you will be the Master.

### -43-
### Two crosses are at the beginning of your Life Line.

You have a very keen sensory apparatus. You perceive things more sharply than most, and often you are preoccupied with satisfying the appetite of your senses. You have laid your intellectual interests to rest and become increasingly materialistic—which you conceal well from others.

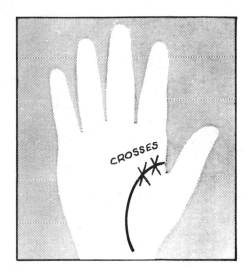

### -44-
### A starred or crossed formation is on your Mount of Venus, inside your Life Line.

Some member of your family agitates you. This person has brought distress and uncertainty into the harmony you are seeking to achieve in your life. This disorder will augment if allowed to continue. Your opponent grows stronger through your submission.

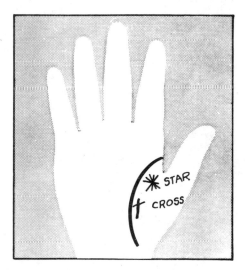

### -45-
### A square is present inside your Life Line on the Mount of Venus.

You long for solitude and peace of mind. You want some privacy and long to escape the rat race, which you find intolerable. Talking it over with allies might unburden you, but you will still carry the heavier load. Everyone wants from you and you have no more to give. You need rejuvenation in your own atmosphere of solace, your haven of solitude into which you can withdraw undisturbed.

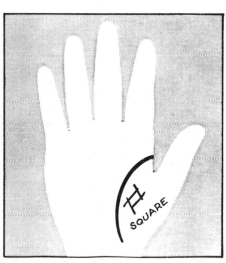

### -46-
### Delicate Hair Lines rise from your Life Line.

Periodically you are supercharged with zesty, strong brain energy. The origin of this force is a mystery to you. Between times you drag yourself around wondering where those beautiful feelings went to, and you feel helpless. At your peak your heart has wings. At your ebb, painful emptiness gnaws at your fiber. Accept your nature and regard the ebb as your time for replenishment, and then you can make the best of both worlds.

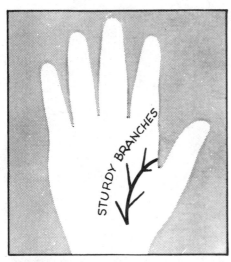

### -47-
### A few small sturdy branches rise upward from your Life Line and point upward.

From time to time you are uplifted with unusual physical courage and mental daring. Physical endurance factors strengthen with the years, feeling better the older you get. Money doesn't flow in regularly. It comes erratically in large sums. The number of upward branches on your Life Line corresponds to the frequency of inflowing money.

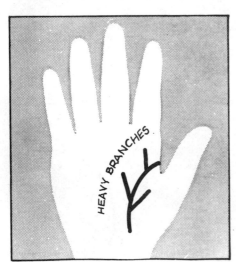

### -48-
### Strong branches part from your Life Line and head upward.

You are a high-spirited, action-packed individual. You feel there is no limit to the things you can accomplish and to the adventures awaiting your exploration. You feel you are on your way to the top of something "big." You attract admirers who linger with you to glean from your enthusiasm and sparkle.

### -49-
### Fine Hair Lines fall downward from your Life Line.

You are at your zenith of your ability to perform great and notable things. Utilize this period of greatest power to resolve all postponed problems. Close the chapters of heartbreaking relationships in your life, as they sap your vital energies. Be as bold as you can be . . . you have it in you. Prove your capableness to higher-ups.

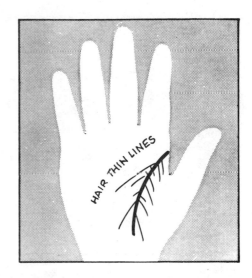

### -50-
### There are small downward-drooping lines off your Life Line.

These are warning signals to protect you from investing money on a hunch. Because you don't examine all the facts and give in to spontaneous impulses, you suffer repeated financial losses. You may fall ill after brooding over losses. You also have the same tendency to fall in love on an impulse and suffer the same letdown. Utilize spare time to break repetitious routines, and surprise yourself by trying new things.

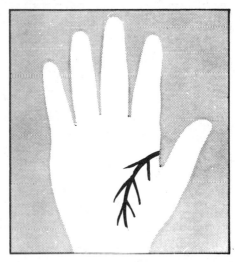

### -51-
### Medium-sized lines curve and drop downward from your Life Line.

Each line represents a passage in your life from a safe and guarded place to a distant and unfamiliar region where you feel threatened and lost. With each move you advance spiritually but lose socially. You regain lost security by gradually making friends and forming lasting relationships with people who are connected to you and appreciate you.

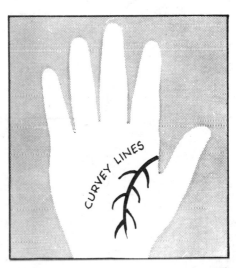

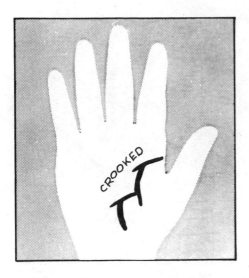

### -52-
### Strong lines drop off your Life Line and force your Life Line into a crooked course.

Long exposure to a lifestyle opposite to your own and years spent away from home have so deeply impressed you that you have grown into a new and different person from what you once were. You yearn for a trusted mentor to guide you in life and to give your life a purpose. A serious course of study will alter your destiny.

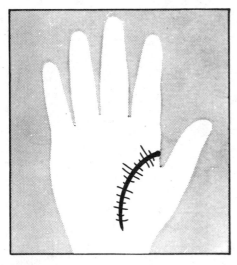

### -53-
### Little fine lines cross your Life Line horizontally.

Your goal is not far off, but unceasing worry blocks your view. Establishing new routines free from habitual worry will clear the way to easy decision-making. Keeping promises is not your forte. You hesitate to commit yourself to new projects, because you worry it will drain your reserves.

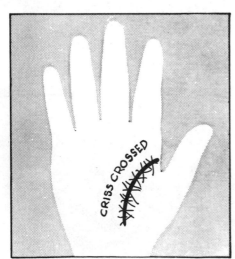

### -54-
### Your Life Line is cut by many little lines going in different directions at once.

You miss feeling fit. You do not easily accept physical discomfort. You are determined to get back to feeling like your own self again. You will feel better by immersing yourself in bright, colorful surroundings, and by involving yourself in activities that you really enjoy. You feel you must be doing something at all times and will often leap into risky ventures just for the sake of doing something.

### -55-
### Thick lines cross over your Life Line.

For as many thick lines that cross over your Life Line, you can count the times you have been significantly injured by others. This happens because you trust others in blind faith and ignore all warning signs. The blows to your pride and reputation do not knock you off your feet, but instead might just harden you into a cynic and plunge you into the depths of resentment. If you can't forget, then accept.

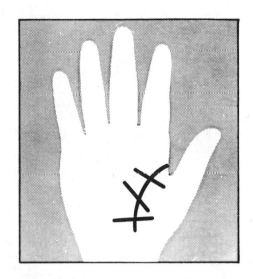

### -56-
### Long lines stemming from the Mount of Venus cut across the Life Line.

You are locking horns with those close to you. Your purposes are crossed, and you are slow to advance. Many personal clashes arise because you frequently go back on your word.

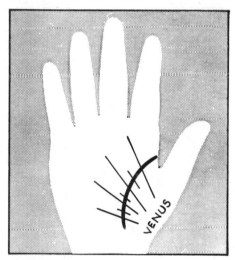

### -57-
### Deep lines from the thumb cut across the Mount of Venus way into the Life Line.

Persons you love and trust could prove treacherous to your personal growth. They could cause losses so great that the wounds would never seem to heal. You must learn to develop an inner light upon which you can meditate to grow strong again.

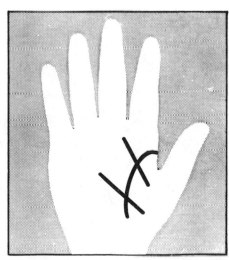

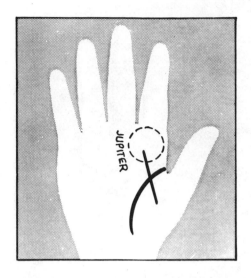

### -58-
### A line from the Mount of Jupiter cuts across your Life Line.

You have a burning desire to reach the highest rank possible in life. You will never be satisfied with just being average. You picture yourself on top, outshining all others. Although your ascent is long and arduous, you will be rewarded earlier than you expect.

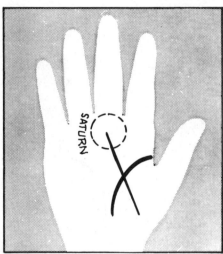

### -59-
### A line runs from your Mount of Saturn and cuts across your Life Line.

You are the sensitive type, with an emotional constitution that needs shielding against insults from others. You are very vulnerable to verbal assaults and should therefore avoid people, including children, who make it a habit of boosting their egos by cutting yours down.

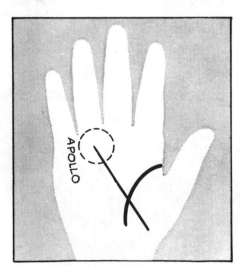

### -60-
### A clear, straight line from the Mount of Apollo cuts across your Life Line onto the Mount of Venus.

One day you will be a widely known person and will be popularly honored for your wealth of talent. Every possible support will be offered you one day by your family and friends, which will boost you to fame.

### -61-
### A clear, direct line from the Mount of Mercury runs across the palm to the Mount of Venus, intersecting your Life Line.

You begin early to play high stakes to win. You work incessantly towards your goal and worry unceasingly about the future. This line indicates that the business ventures you worry about most turn out in your favor. Wealth and status make you happy. Your spell of good luck might break if you do not give thanks where thanks is due.

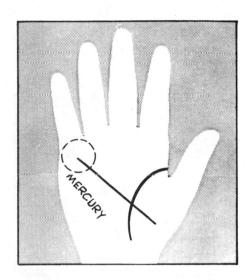

### -62-
### A line cuts across your Life Line from the Mount of Moon to the Mount of Venus.

You have experienced some bad luck with the opposite sex. Now you have developed unnecessary fears about deeper involvements. If you let past disappointments be your guide, you will only get more lonely. You are disappointed more easily than others because of an early injury to your feelings that just refuses to heal.

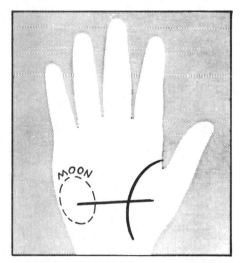

### -63-
### A line travels across both your Life and Head Lines alike.

Sorrow has confused you, and so have vexations from a meddling relative who had handcuffed your life. This relative means well and is sometimes right and sometimes generous . . . but you can't take the suppression any more. Be a soldier and dare to be yourself, and you will feel lighter and merrier.

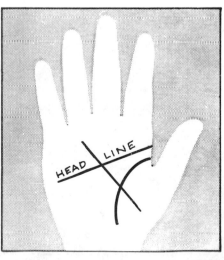

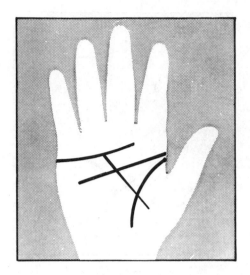

### -64-
**A line starting anywhere on your Life Line cuts across your Head Line and terminates exactly on your Heart Line.**

This line can be curved to the right or left or be straight. It means there is an old misunderstanding between you and a close relative that has been gnawing at you for years. You are afraid to address it. Although your adversary disrespects and incriminates you, you pretend it doesn't happen. This person should be subdued.

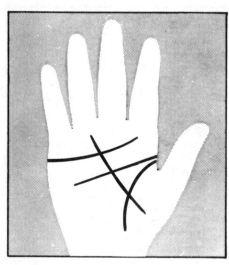

### -65-
**A sweeping line (curved or straight) cuts across your Life and Head Lines and through your Heart Line.**

On more than one occasion relatives have meddled in your life. They have begrudged your choice of partner. There will never be a meeting of minds about your personal freedom. To be free to fly away with the one you love, never expect to look back and see your relatives' heads nodding with approval.

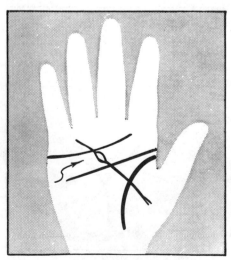

### -66-
**An island formation is on the line (curved or straight) which cuts across your Heart, Head, and Life Lines.**

You enter a love affair, which in the beginning promises the stars. Towards the end you will be trapped in an atmosphere of accusation and guilt. This guilt might follow you into future relationships, and only with great effort will you be able to break this pattern.

### -67-
### A line from the Mount of Venus crosses your Life Line and intersects your Apollo Line.

A longstanding discrepancy comes to a head between you and a relative. Your adversary, although you were never aware of it, was never a friend. The outcome of the proceedings (if it goes to court) will be initially a disappointment. Much later will things turn in your favor.

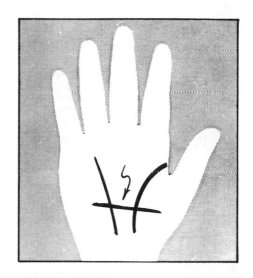

### -68-
### Your Life Line sends an upward branch towards the Mount of Jupiter.

You hold your head high. You put forth a constant effort to assert yourself and look good. You have little patience for the slow and dull. You are quick-tempered when challenged. You are capable of quickly rising to power once you determine your direction. You search for goals of light burden.

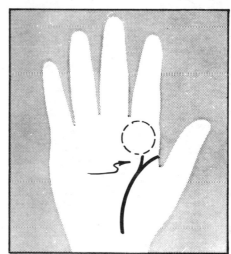

### -69-
### An ascending line from your Life Line covers your Mount of Jupiter.

This is the mark of achievement of a great master and teacher. The bearer of this mark rises to success because of a dynamic attraction to the right people. They point the way and remove obstacles. This coincides with augmented success through schooling and a position of authority over others. Keep sights off of material rewards and your mark will be in history.

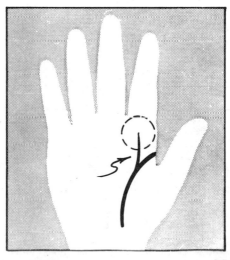

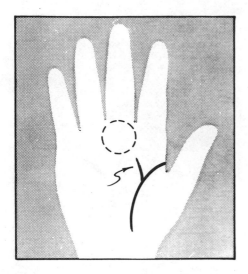

### -70-
### An ascending branch from your Life Line runs towards the Mount of Saturn.

You have taught yourself many trades and struggled alone to go places while everyone held you back. You know now that you cannot depend upon family to stand behind career plans. You are often left to do the cleanup job. You can always fall back on the inner resource of your talents to give you strength.

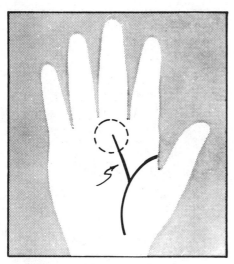

### -71-
### A rising line from your Life Line runs over the Mount of Saturn.

This denotes acquisition of real estate. Also other tangible assets carry you through periods of hardship. Another interpretation for this line is that a secret is locked inside of you and the key was thrown away. The secret is gradually unraveled through a series of coincidences, starting out by meeting a stranger who cares. You gain enlightenment by solving this enigma and are carried into a second fate—a new life—a life of positive rewards.

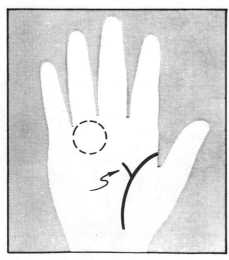

### -72-
### A branch from your Life Line points to the Mount of Apollo.

It's a lucky sign that your talents will catch the judge's eye. Waste no time in entering contests. Awards, prizes, and popularity follow suit. This is an omen of success in the hands of people in show business, in public service, in law, and in the arts. Money also comes to those with this sign, often from out of the blue.

### -73-
### A line from your Life Line ascends to Mercury.

This promises early success in business. You will rise faster than most to a position of authority. You are accomplished in many fields. This makes it difficult for you to settle down and choose one specialty. You may have several professions in succession. You fare equally well in whichever field you specialize. Your rewards endure till old age.

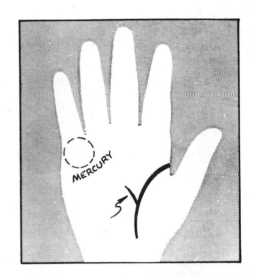

### -74-
### A line ascends from your Life Line and runs to your Upper Mars.

A person in high position helps you to shape up for a fight that will fulfill a great longing. You develop moral courage to face fearsome events undaunted. Your heart is the seat of your intelligence; that is, your first impulse is to act emotionally, then rationally, when solving problems.

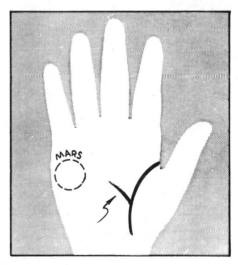

### -75-
### Your Life Line ends in a small fork.

You are tearing yourself apart with ruminations about an impossible decision. You are damned if you do and damned if you don't. While you are deadlocked, look for an interesting diversion until the solution is at hand. Act on first impulse when the ice breaks, just to get momentum.

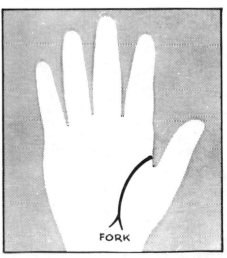

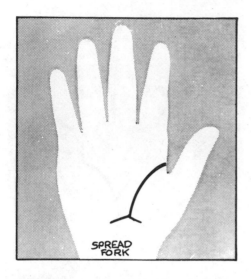

### -76-
### Your Life Line divides at the end in a wide-spreading fork.

Close family ties and steady companionship are not that essential to you. You make a point of doing routine things very differently than others. You have a fascination for foreign places and a burning desire to set up your life in an exotic place.

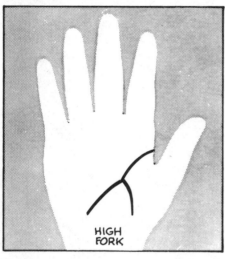

### -77-
### There is a fork in your Life Line that begins in about the center of the hand.

You are always on the go. Your restless nature leads you to wander away from secure surroundings in search of the ultimate place free from stress. A restraint imposed upon you over a period of years has made you restless. Once you rediscover your purpose, all your old strength will come back.

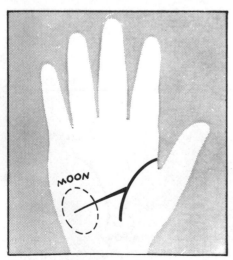

### -78-
### A fork from your Life Line ends on the Mount of the Moon.

You yearn to travel, and if you can't get away, your imagination takes you there. You have travel in your blood and would do well in the travel industry. You are excitable and are the kind of person who can hardly wait for things. Since your enthusiasm can be catching, you would be great on a TV game show.

### -79-
### A split line forking down from your Life Line descends to the Mount of the Moon.

You are careless about your belongings and sometimes your appearance. This started out as a minor problem in childhood and keeps growing. At home, valuables fossilize in special hiding places because you can no longer remember where you placed them. Your mind is often absorbed in loftier thoughts, hence your carelessness.

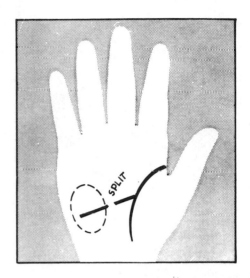

### -80-
### There is a line branching downward from your Life Line, and it ends in an island formation.

You are a frustrated explorer. You are easily bored, so you turn to dreaming of adventure. Trips requiring extensive preparation usually disappoint you. You are a spur-of-the-moment person. Avoid chaos on the road by choosing a partner with mutual interests.

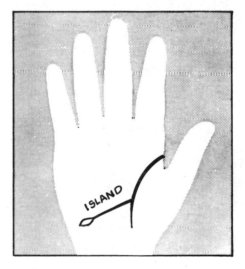

### -81-
### There is a square on a line branching downward from the Life Line.

Bon Voyage! You find escape from boredom in travel. The square, a protection sign, gives you the courage to venture far from home. Deep inside you always know you will arrive home safely. You are just as relaxed anywhere in the world as you are in your own living room.

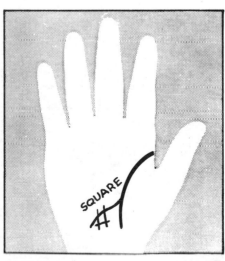

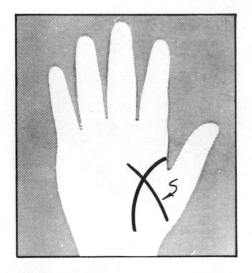

### -82-
### An interference line from your thumb attacks the Life Line.

An unfavorable liason from your early life appears without invitation to haunt you about past differences. Be rid of the pesty individual tactfully, but as swiftly as possible. The confrontation is inevitable. Serious setbacks are suffered if you pick up where you left off.

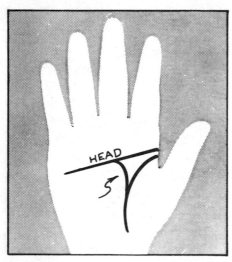

### -83-
### An ascending line from your Life Line stops at the Head Line.

You discover the true nature of your life's destination. You begin to accept yourself for what you are, recognizing limitations and taking pride in assets. This comes as a welcome relief after a long period of bewilderment. With this you become an independent thinker and learn to rely less upon the opinions of others.

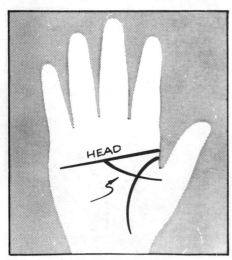

### -84-
### An interference line from your thumb cuts across the Life Line and stops at the Head Line.

A person whom you rely upon and admire forces you to assume their way of thinking. Don't let anyone rob you of your self-image. When you feel manipulated, find immediate release and strengthen your mental image of powerfulness. Because of your vulnerable self-image, you must forget past failures and start afresh every day by trusting in yourself.

### -85-
### An interference line from your thumb cuts across the Life Line and attacks your Heart Line.

Meddlesome party, envious of your happiness, spreads ugly rumor to turn others against you. The truth comes out. Keep no secrets. Clear up those old misunderstandings. An affair interferes with a special mission. Don't accept a false goal to impress others.

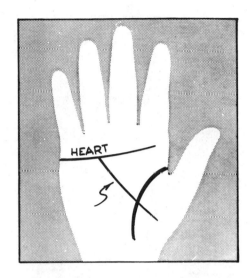

### -86-
### An ascending line from your Life Line is stopped by your Fate Line.

A final decision is made after years of deliberation . . . you break free from conditions that oppressed you. You connect with your true fate in life through your involvement with a concerned friend. This person helps you to catch a ride to success. Your trust in life is restored.

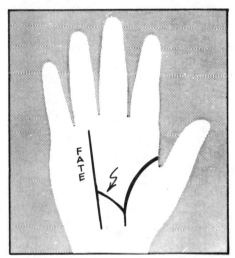

### -87-
### An ascending line from your Life Line runs parallel with your Fate Line.

Events in your life are forever running the way everybody else would like them to. You let others plan your life. You feel helpless in your career and in your love life. Life is teaching you the hard lesson of patience. You feel life is sliding by and you are being left behind. Once you begin planning your own life and deciding things for yourself, your fears will subside.

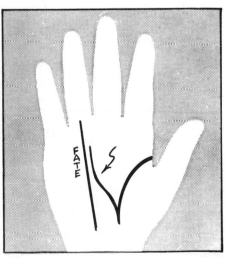

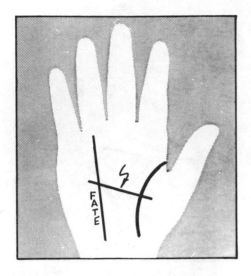

### -88-
**An interference line from your thumb crosses the Life Line and attacks the Fate Line, crossing over it.**

Opponents in business scene unite forces and seem to lash out against you. You are an unusual person, and are different in so many ways that the average person can't accept your individuality. To get around this you will have to bluff others into believing you are like them until they accept you.

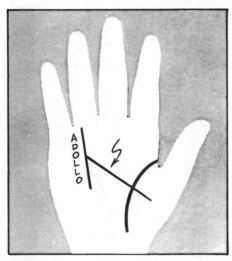

### -89-
**An interference line from the thumb cuts across your Life Line and attacks the Line of Apollo.**

A scandal caused by the ignorance of others penetrates deep into your psyche. The scandal will pass, everyone will forget, but the memory lingers and possesses you. A stranger extricates you from an intrigue. You cannot hold a secret.

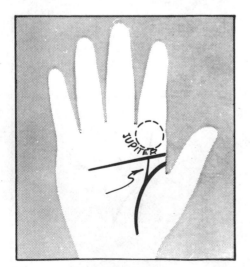

### -90-
**An ascending line from the Life Line heads towards Jupiter but is stopped by the Head Line.**

You look for opportunity after it has knocked. If only you were more daring you could catch a few of those lucky trains that whiz by. Boredom enters career. You must fight it off by developing new interests and through physical-type activities.

### -91-
### Two little branches from your Life Line ascend to connect with the Head Line.

Your parents gave you a good start in life, and your childhood had more happiness in it than most. You expect your parents' support forever and have a hard time breaking the cord. Don't count on an inheritance or free monies until the latter part of your life. For now you have to keep your nose to the grindstone. Your level of tolerance for annoyance is high, although you don't feel it is.

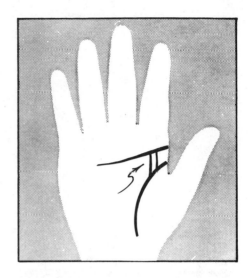

### -92-
### An ascending line from the Life Line extends to your Lower Mars.

You have been put to the test for a very long time. Supporters select you as the likely candidate for an important job. Suffering and endless waiting period subside. Your yearning to bathe in public esteem is realized by special privileges in the second half of your life.

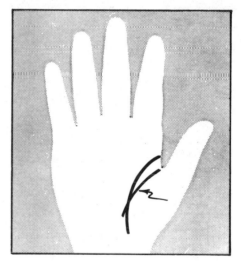

# MARS LINE

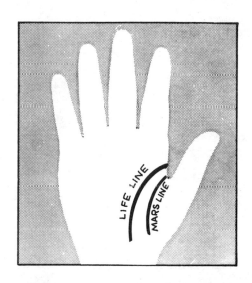

### -93-
**Your Line of Mars encircles the thumb inside the Life Line.**

This is an excellent sign, giving you vitality and resilience in the face of adversity and illness. It reinforces a weak Life Line, thus minimizing danger and evil. It is an excellent sign to carry if you follow a dangerous or stressful calling.

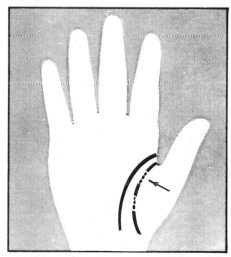

### -94-
**Your Mars Line fades out, but renews itself later.**

A person of strong influence in your life ceases his or her involvement for a time. The reason is not revealed. You can be strong standing alone, but this requires a strong belief in yourself. A new self-confidence can be gained here. Once your association with the aforesaid person is renewed, you become a stronger individual.

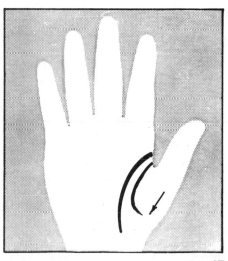

### -95-
**Your Mars Line travels for a while parallel to the Life Line and retreats inward towards the base of the thumb.**

This sign indicates that integral to your survival will be the need to break completely free from the past. Cherish your old friends, but make a steady stream of new ones. A person closely allied with you from early years wishes to break ties. Be gentle and forgiving. Loved one will always love you, no matter what happens.

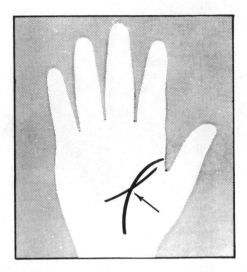

### -96-
### Your Mars Line cuts through your Life Line.

Home life has a worrisome atmosphere. Family members oppose your views. Harassment ensues. Relatives have nailed you into a corner and stopped you from going your own way. You have lost trust in yourself and are afraid to go it alone financially. Valuable time is lost in brooding and worrying over things that cannot be changed. Prepare for a constructive change and follow through.

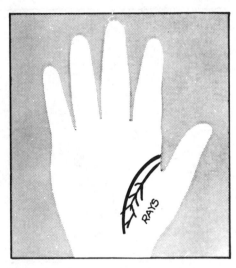

### -97-
### Your Mars Line has numerous ray-like projections.

LOVE is the word you like to hear most, especially repeated day and night by the one you love. LOVE is your daily bread. You need constant reassurance and affection to keep your spirits high. You are considered old-fashioned in love, and can only be passionate if you trust your partner 100 percent.

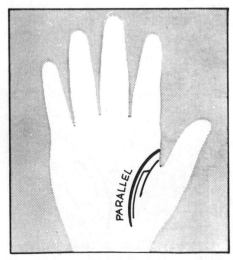

### -98-
### Your Mars Line sends a ray line parallel to your Life Line.

A gentle person enters your life at an early age. This person is partially responsible for shaping your personality. You become sensitively aware of the precious gift of life. You strive to become peace-loving and compassionate, and with age you begin to take on a peaceful feeling inside.

### -99-
### Your Mars Line sends several ray lines to intersect your Life Line.

You might be haunted every now and again by an unfavorable association from your wilder days. You did some capricious things in your youth. This person enjoys reminding you of your past. This individual no longer has the goods on you, so you can walk away and need not be upset.

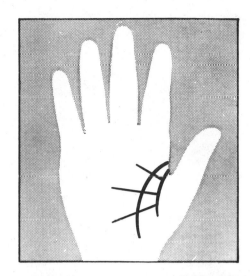

### -100-
### Your Mars Line sends a ray line straight across to the Life Line.

A third party sends a Ray Line straight across your most tender parts and tries to sever you from a loved one. Seeds of suspicion are planted. It is time to wage war, fight for your life and the one you love. Reestablish closeness with loved one and use all excess energies to combat this meddlesome party.

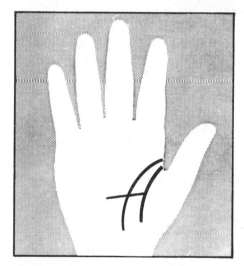

### -101-
### Your Mars Line sends a ray line cutting across the Life Line to the Mount of Mars.

Listen to the advice of those who know you better. A slight habit of yours could become a serious addiction. Ventilate your feelings promptly, sparing injury to loved ones. Don't hold in those feelings of hostility. Confidence in a stranger solves a problem of long standing. Combat your restlessness through usefulness.

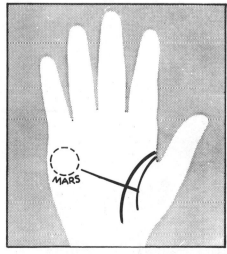

# HEAD LINE

### -102-
### Your Head Line is straight.

You advance amidst the struggles of life using the sound judgment of an uncluttered mind. You know how to turn adversities in your favor. You can always find something to laugh about while others are being grim. That streak of conventionality underlying your makeup is what keeps you afloat.

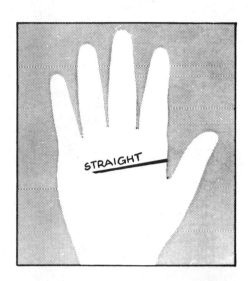

### -103-
### Your Head Line is long.

This denotes extreme economy due to reason and calculation. You search for the quickest, most efficient ways to get things done. You want to live forever. You like to do things as fast as possible. A tremendous intensity of character enables you to get what you set your heart on. Due to your intense need to be in control at all times you sometimes paralyze friendships.

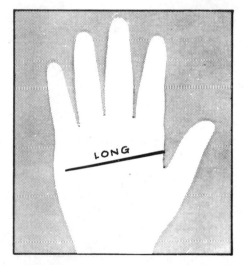

### -104-
### Your Head Line travels straight across the palm, practically meeting both ends.

You have superabundant intelligence and excel in analytical deliberations. Your mind is outfitted to do extremely well in commerce, industry, or finance. You are proud of your brains. Since you are sometimes "above" others, try not to bore them. High-risk financial practices tempt you.

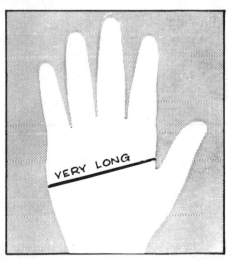

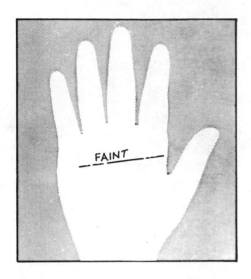

### -105-
### Your Head Line is weakly developed.

This suggests a lack of purpose or ambition in this period of your life. This might be a temporary setback due to a personal upset. Natural drives return after a spell of diversion. If you are feeling weak and tired, not so much rest as successful accomplishments will refresh you.

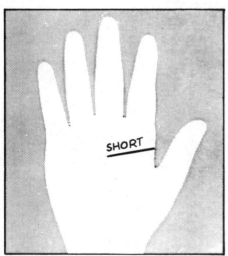

### -106-
### Your Head Line is short.

You are a creature of habit. You respect the tangible, the concrete. At last you've lost your pipe dreams. You enjoy getting all those odd jobs out of the way before you begin your daily routine. This routine is essential for you, because it provides security and reduces anxiety about the future.

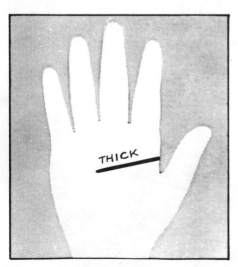

### -107-
### Your Head Line is thickly developed.

It is a sign of not applying your powers of concentration to their fullest. You do not lack potential, you merely lack organization. In trying to stabilize your vacillating nature, you may choose to work things out physically. The "physical" you is stronger than the "mental" you. A robust, outdoor life is just what you need right now.

### -108-
### Your Head Line is accompanied by a sister line.

These are rare and fortunate creases to have. It expresses a dual mentality. One side of you is extremely cautious, the other is self-confident with a great desire to rule others. You are capable of enormous mental work. An inheritance rescues you in time of distress.

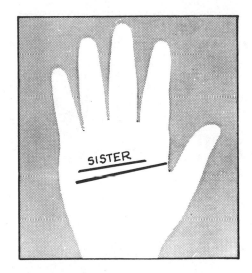

### -109-
### Your Head Line is interrupted by gaps and clear breaks.

This indicates that you have recently experienced a disappointment of the heart. This experience brought you into a state of imbalance. Healing comes swiftly when you fill those spaces with good feelings and reconnect them with new friendships.

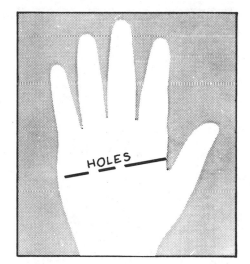

### -110-
### Your Head Line has a broken ladder-like structure.

Your life lacks stability. You are sometimes fickle, shifting your attitudes whimsically. Often you fly off on tangents and pursue the impractical and the unreliable. Your peers are watching your every move and waiting for decisive, mature action on your part. But there is a wild buck in you that still needs to play.

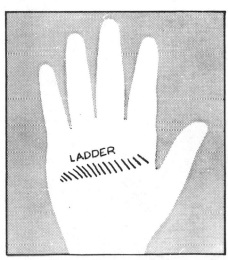

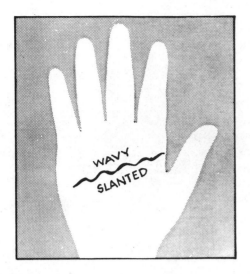

### -111-
### Your Head Line is wavy and slanted.

The melancholy part of your character is very obvious. Sometimes you wonder if you ever had one completely happy day in your life. You see grief and suffering where others don't. You've found that staying alone brings you the least grief. You are miserly about spending time on developing friendships.

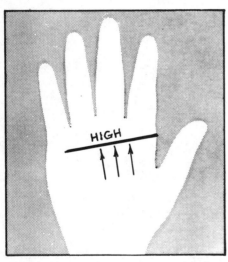

### -112-
### Your Head Line rises high on the palm.

You develop an enormous fixity of purpose. You develop your "stick-to-it-iveness" to accomplish a goal that you keep secret. You deliberately control your affections and will not let affairs of the heart get in the way of your success. Great intellectual endeavors are not always yours, but a vehement nature found in connection with this marking is.

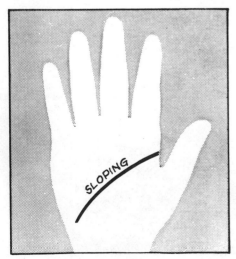

### -113-
### You have a long, slightly sloping Head Line.

In all practical matters of life you show foresight. You are aware of your unusually high mental progress, your fine memory, and strong powers of visualization. You are putting forth constant effort to improve yourself. In everything you do, you feel you should be learning something new.

### -114-
### Your Head Line is chained.

You have not as yet come to final maturity. Although you feel mature, there is a lot of work still ahead of you. Sometimes you need to be prodded and coaxed to move along. It is also indicated that if you cherish a more generous spirit towards others, you will grow faster inwardly.

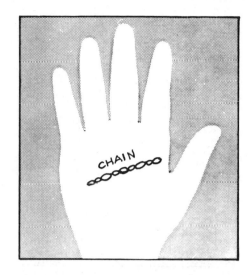

### -115-
### Your Head Line rises on the end towards the Mount of Mercury.

You are a very precise individual, paying close attention to externals. You have the talent to express your ridicule and dissatisfaction by subtle imitation. You are aggressive, and you hide it. You use the mimicry as protection.

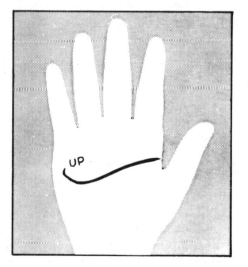

### -116-
### A line off your Head Line branches downward towards the Mount of the Moon.

You cannot always be relied upon to keep things in confidence. Even if it's expected of you, you just can't keep silent. You are compelled by a force stronger than you are to "tell all." You have an easygoing nature which others criticize as lazy. You are looking for someone whom you can rely on, who can be gentle, and who doesn't scold.

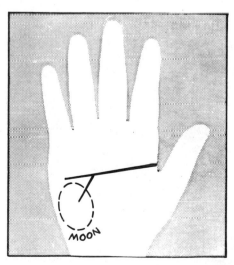

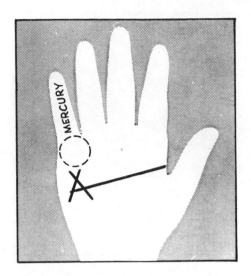

### -117-
### There is a triangle on your Head Line under Mercury.

You are a careful, diligent person who studiously inquires into the meaning of all things. You get satisfaction from paying attention to detail and puzzling the mysteries of life together. Your aim is to discover new facts and interpret them to make the world better. You would make a good scientist.

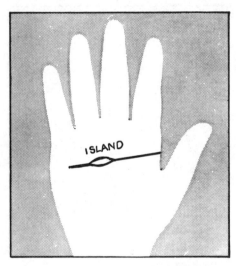

### -118-
### An island is situated on your Head Line.

You could be a workaholic. Something is causing you to work too hard and too long, almost to the point of exhaustion. You tend to work in an excited or confused state. You don't know when you are overdoing it, but afterwards you feel it.

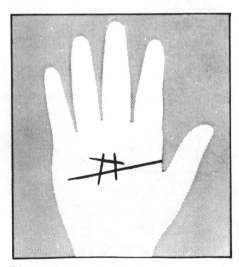

### -119-
### A square is present on your Head Line.

Your intuition saves you from a string of misfortunes. The square protects you from the bad outcome of future misfortunes, but does not protect you from getting into them in the first place. You attract bad fortune, because you are used to it; it is all you know. Now you need to be reprogrammed to accept good fortune.

### -120-
### Your Head Line arches towards the Mount of Jupiter, then gently resumes its course.

You achieve what you set out to, because you never take "no" for an answer. You are stubbornly pushing your way forward. You have chosen a goal of high standards. You are tough and cannot be beaten, not by anyone.

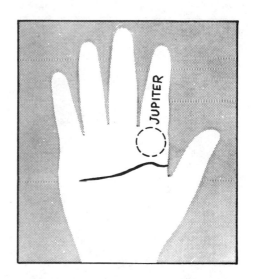

### -121-
### There is a deflection of your Head Line under Saturn.

Your mental world is Saturnian. You immerse yourself in books and reflections. Your studies take you away from the everyday realities, which you view as glum and hopeless. You seek wisdom, and one day soon you will work out your own private solution for happiness.

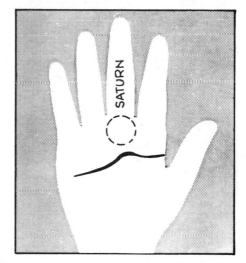

### -122-
### Your Head Line deflects towards Apollo.

This means you assume the mental life of the Apollonian. You are never afraid to air your views. If you practice being more disciplined, you will avoid conflicts. You tend to say things that pop into your head without screening them first. Be more secretive. Learn to relax more. You know what you want but let yourself be easily discouraged.

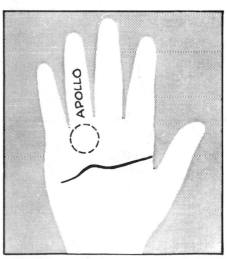

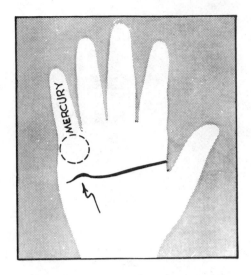

### -123-
### There is a deflection of your Head Line under Mercury.

Your mental life leans heavily towards the Mercurial way of thinking. You are a shrewd thinker and a wise judge of character. Your energy is almost tireless. Mentally you grasp and retain things more easily than most. You are the master of the art of saying the right thing at the right time.

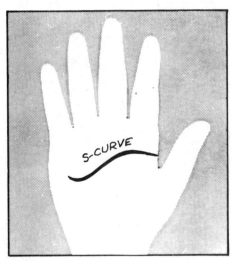

### -124-
### Your Head Line is S-curved.

Your practical and imaginative sides stand in conflict with one another. Your conscience forces you to be practical and is fighting for first place with your creative imagination. You consider it indulgent to spend time developing a new hobby, but it is exactly what you need. Your body needs the healing and palliative powers of a creative hobby.

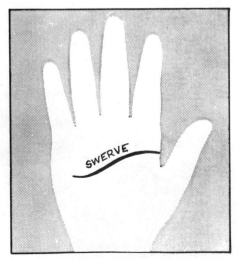

### -125-
### Your Head Line has a slight swerve in it.

Some unusual strain has been forced upon you. Through a practical action and a turn of mind, you rise superior to the occasion. The ordeal that upset you becomes a vague memory, but makes you wiser and richer in the business of living. It is possible for you to learn to react less emotionally and avoid stressing your body.

### -126-
### Your Head Line runs a wavy, twisted course.

You are wavering, changeable and easily irritated. Lately, you find it hard to make up your mind, and afterwards you worry about having made the wrong decision. To succeed you must be tougher with yourself. Let no one be an audience to your indecision. Be determined (even if you must fake it), and others will begin to heed your word.

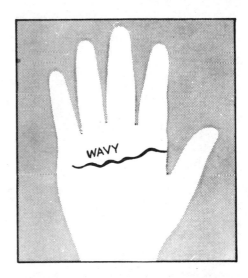

### -127-
### Your Head Line ends in a small, neat fork.

This means you have the "gift of gab" and a keen insight into rational thinking. Your aptitude for using and understanding words makes you well-suited for the legal profession. As a persuasive talker you can explain your way through life. You see problems from multiple viewpoints, which makes you a fair judge.

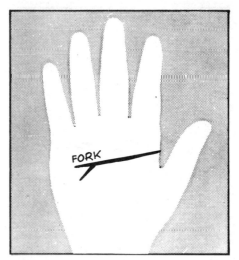

### -128-
### Your Head Line ends with a strong fork.

You are able to view both sides of an issue fairly before passing judgment. Your personality has extra vigor because of these dual assets of practical and imaginative thinking. You detest narrow-mindedness. You have a calling to be in an acting (theatrical) setting. This marking is often found in the hands of comedians.

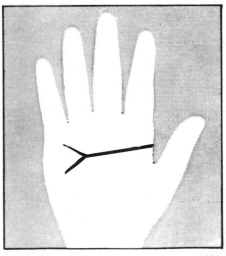

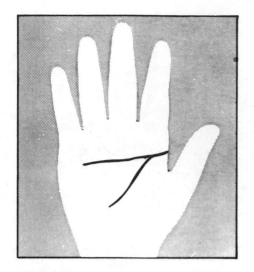

### -129-
### Your Head Line begins to fork at the very start.

You have a dual nature, switching between the introvert type and the extrovert type. You could vacillate from being feverishly religious one day to being a bitter agnostic the next. You live two lives—one under God, and one against God. You assume two manners of conversation, changing to suit the occasion— one friendly and one fierce.

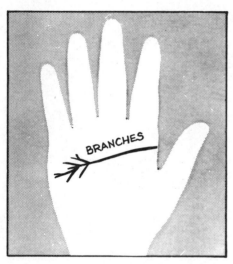

### -130-
### Your Head Line has a multiple fork at the end.

You are versatile and adapt to changing life situations like a chameleon. Normally you don't mind moving, and feel comfortable in strange places. You are a fighter, and if you don't have anything to fight for, you turn it inward against yourself. You block your own achievements by pure procrastination.

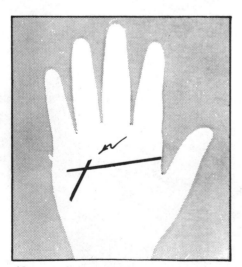

### -131-
### Your Head Line is interrupted by a slanting line near the end.

This sign means you have not been true to yourself. You do not see yourself objectively. Others mock you, mistaking your humility and quietness for meekness. Don't downgrade your abilities. You can still excel in anything you want to do.

### -132-
### A single line from Jupiter joins your Head Line.

Ambitious thoughts fill your mind. You work hard for what you believe in. Once you believe in something, nothing can change your mind. You want to see your name in lights. If you let it, foolishness of heart could destroy your business profits.

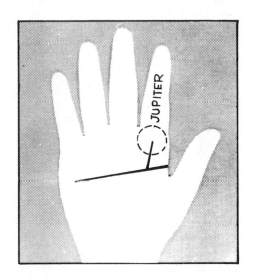

### -133-
### A line arises under Saturn and attaches itself to the Head Line.

Your thoughts are Saturnine: concern for others, sometimes sluggish, careful, cynical. Your attributes are wisdom and understanding human nature. You are studious and precise. You reserve your opinions mostly for yourself, because you believe that nothing you say or do could ever change the world.

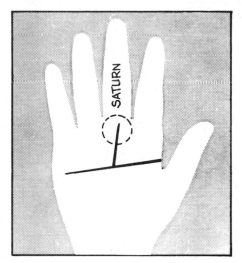

### -134-
### A branch from your Head Line proceeds to the Mount of Apollo.

An artistic, creative, or literary talent is about to lead you to recognition and give you that financial reward you've been expecting. Success arrives at that point when you combine practicality with your artwork.

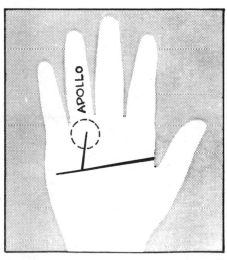

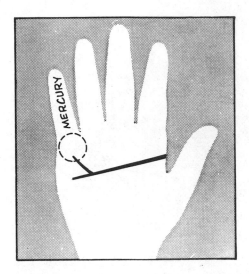

### -135-
### A line from Mercury splits and joins your Head Line.

Your thoughts run in Mercurial channels. You are fascinated by the scientific method of doing things, and you use it in your business. You calculate your business affairs well in advance, and know through rehearsal precisely what to say. You are intuitive. You react as a barometer in direct measure to how others treat you.

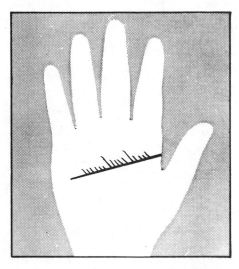

### -136-
### Numerous small lines arise from your Head Line and point upward.

This shows you are constantly aspiring to rise above your present status and improve socially and personally. You are receptive to suggestions concerning ways to better your life. Numerous small defeats along the way do not lessen your chance for success.

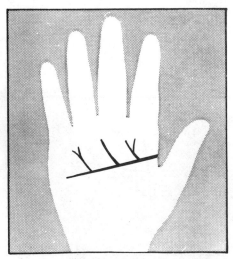

### -137-
### There are strong branches arising from your Head Line pointing upward.

This indicates that your mind is in a state of confusion due to the many unexpected events that took you by surprise. People enter your life as helpers handing out fool's advice. Your thoughts might wander in bewilderment. Break free of all troublesome persons who chastise you.

### -138-
### Small branches drop off your Head Line and point downward.

You are easily discouraged and do not fight the battle of life with all the vigor within you. You brainwash yourself into believing you are unlucky. You tire mainly because of tenseness and negative thinking in your daily routine.

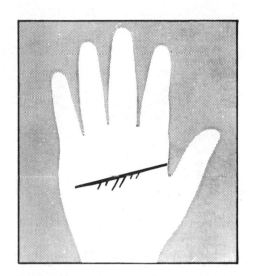

### -139-
### You have a short line branching down off the Head Line.

Developing your imaginative faculties should be an issue of foremost importance in your life. Through innovation in a business maneuver, you could prosper enough to afford much-desired leisure time. In retirement years you develop a new talent and profit from it.

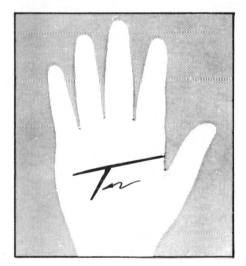

### -140-
### Your Head Line begins on the Mount of Jupiter and follows a normal course.

Your thoughts are turned inward. You scrutinize your actions. As a student of psychology, you are adept at handling people of all ages. You are a convincing speaker and have rapport as a leader. People sense your self-confidence and rely upon you for direction. You dictate with gentle firmness.

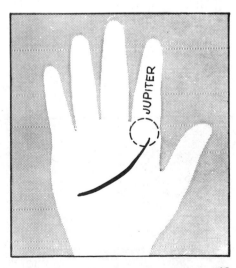

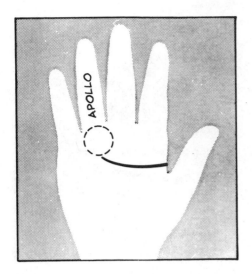

### -141-
### Your Head Line curves towards the Mount of Apollo.

Apollo, which strongly influences your actions, can bring you celebrity or riches—the choice is yours. Apollo is the representative of the Arts, and has given you a taste for literature and music. You are also the professional showman type . . . your smile causes others to shine; your joy is infectious.

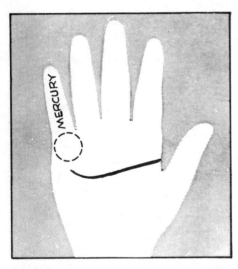

### -142-
### Your Head Line bends upward towards Mercury.

Your life is inspired by a force called Mercury. Mercury gives you appreciation of science, knowledge of business, responsibilities, and an honorable carriage. The core of you is materialistic. You operate with skilled and tireless energy. You are intellectually curious about making big money, and have some talent along this line. You make many sacrifices in the name of money.

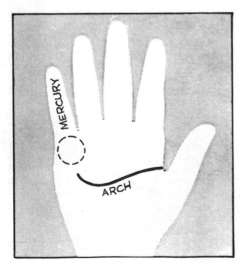

### -143-
### Your Head Line arches towards the Mount of Mercury.

This denotes that the older you become the greater your interest will be for money and possessions. With every year your desire for money and comfort grows stronger, and obligations press. Your determination alone makes you rich. Enjoy the freedom of your youth, as it might be the price you pay for riches.

### -144-
### Your Head Line ends on the upper Mount of Mars.

This shows that the common-sense side of your personality dominates. You have a fistful of practical solutions for everyday problems. You are a careful observer. You can enjoy pleasure vicariously with others, and you do not begrudge their happiness.

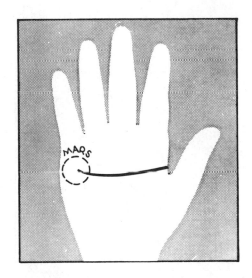

### -145-
### Your Head Line slopes gradually towards the Mount of the Moon.

This reveals your artistic, creative mind. Your richly endowed imaginative forces attract admirers who patronize you. You are self-sufficient, methodical, and organized. You could write fiction, poetry, or give speeches.

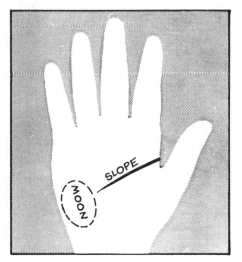

### -146-
### After your Head Line has crossed the Plane of Mars, it proceeds to the Mount of the Moon.

You gladly forfeit some of your sound judgment to view the world artistically and idealistically. Your fantasies push reality aside. Your extravagant, unrestrained imagination sometimes stampedes into furious adventure.

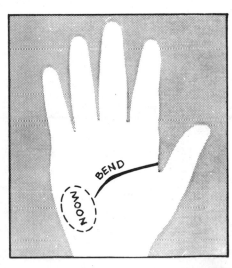

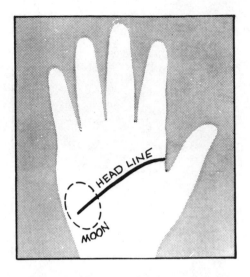

### -147-
### Your Head Line projects very far down into the Mount of the Moon.

You have an inclination towards mysticism. Occult documents intrigue you. In the magic of the "unexplained" you lose yourself. You dream of becoming a mystic or a psychic. Once you start exploring the field, you will discover that you have laudable psychic powers.

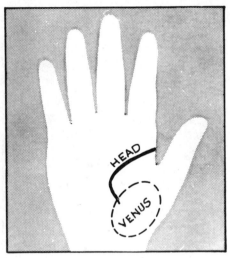

### -148-
### Your Head Line curves around and ends on the Mount of Venus.

This is a rare sign. Your mind is attracted to Venusian ideas. This means you are filled with sympathy and love. You inspire love in others. Your warmth continually attracts the opposite sex. Here you have a hard time restraining yourself.

# HEAD LINE JOINED TO LIFE LINE

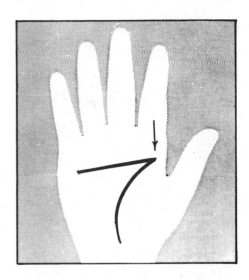

### -149-
**Your Head Line is joined to your Life Line, which rises under Jupiter.**

You are a highly evolved, sensitive person inclined to be deficient in self-control. You habitually sell yourself short, and forget to reward yourself for a job well done. You get yourself locked into very uncomfortable situations, and stay locked in because you are needlessly afraid to break loose.

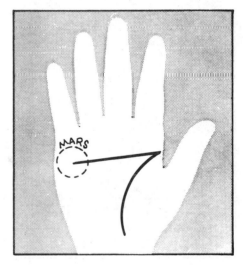

### -150-
**Your Head and Life Lines are joined, and the Head Line runs straight across the palm, stopping at the Mount of Mars.**

This implies that you overreact to irritations because you are hypersensitive. To compensate for your sensitivity, you hide your true feelings and come across to others forcefully. As a result, your friends do not recognize you as a sensitive person, but as a dominant one.

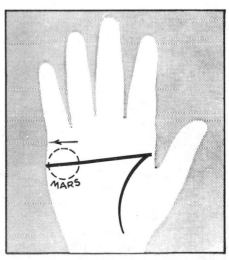

### -151-
**Your Head and Life Lines are joined, and the Head Line runs across the palm over the Mount of Mars.**

This indicates you are an extremely strong-minded and determined individual. Because of the joined lines at the beginning, you are beneath it all the sensitive, serious type, flinching at any criticism. The length of your Head Line marks you as a person who can conceal vulnerabilities. Your sense of duty compels you to sacrifice for what you believe in.

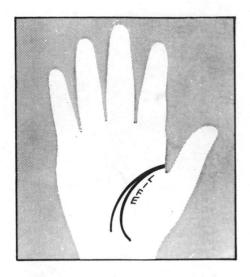

### -152-
### Your Head Line is joined to the Life Line at the start and curves down around and follows it.

This form is largely found in the hands of artists or persons who appreciate and understand the arts. If you have not as yet developed some artistic talent to its fullest, you definitely should do so. Some of your thinking is of a dark sort with a gloomy note. You need your artistic musings to offset this.

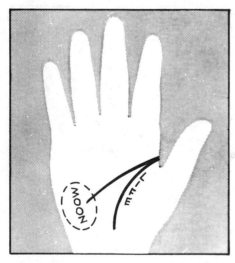

### -153-
### Your Head Line is joined to the Life Line at the start, and the Head Line slopes downward onto the Mount of the Moon.

This is a distinctive mark of people who exercise conscious control over their emotions. Often you are inhibited, unable to express to others what you really mean and want. You hold your feelings back for long periods of time, and then suddenly something bursts, and you are free again.

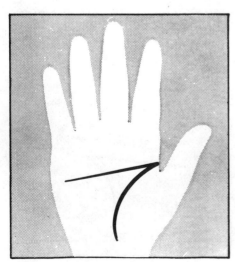

### -154-
### Your Head Line and Life Line separate immediately after a common origin.

This shows a healthy element of caution in your personality. You proceed cautiously in dealings with others. You are restrained. You test them for your acceptance. You hate having others at your heels and are sensitively aware when others enter your "space bubble." You are vulnerable to the mischief of others. It is advised you keep distant from those with whom you do not feel safe.

### -155-
**Your Life Line and Head Line begin as one line, which remains joined well into the Plane of Mars.**

Your friends see you as an extremely cautious, reticent individual. There is an element of suspicion throughout your personality, which you sometimes use as a protective mechanism to guard your sore spots.

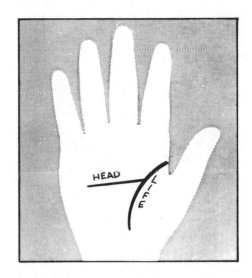

### -156-
**Your Head Line does not leave the Life Line until nearly the middle of the Life Line.**

In this case you will probably not develop into an independent thinker until you are well on in life. Independent thinking on your part now would mean breaking away from relatives and friends who have forged your life until now. No matter how controlled you feel, you still need them. You are destined to make it on your own, sooner or later.

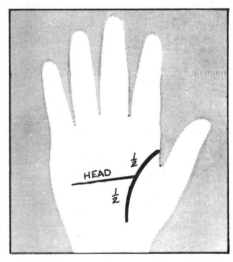

### -157-
**Your Head Line and Life Line are joined and affixed high on the palm under the index finger.**

You are a subtle abstract thinker. You like to play with the logical arrangement of things. Quick to grasp new concepts, you leave old ones behind. With your sharp wit and excellent sense of humor, you would make an excellent teacher.

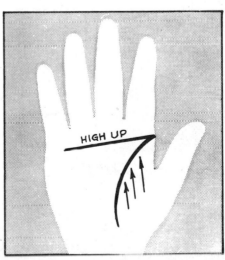

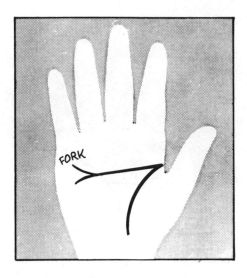

### -158-
**Your Head Line, which is joined to the Life Line at the start, is forked at the end.**

This forked mark symbolizes an insufficient ability to make quick decisions. You try very hard to balance between being practical and being imaginative. Your reaction time is delayed because of your indecisive nature. When in doubt, act according to first impulse. You waste important time analyzing the nature of the problems you face.

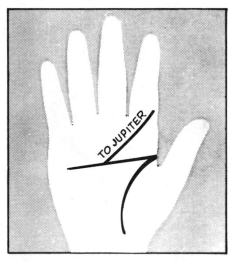

### -159-
**Your Head Line rises from your Life Line, and a branch off the Head Line rises to Jupiter.**

You are ruled by an ambition to be a great person. You enjoy explaining things to people and are a natural-born leader. Some of your friends admire your sureness, and less adoring ones find you boring, so forget them. Your interests are out of the ordinary.

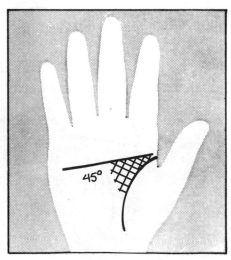

### -160-
**The Supreme Angle formed below your index finger by your Head Line and Life Line is clear, sharp, and under 45 degrees.**

You were born with a gentle, fair disposition. You are of noble nature . . . a friend to all. Sometimes you butter up people to make them like you more. Some people do not appreciate your kindly nature.

### -161-
### The Supreme Angle formed by the meeting of your Life Line and Head Line is larger than 45 degrees.

You have a hard time understanding what others want and expect from you. Therefore it is not easy for you to please people, although you mean well. You are not always able to place yourself in another person's position to understand their viewpoint.

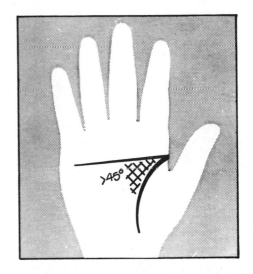

### -162-
### There is a short outside fork at the start of your Head Line.

You are a person of scruples and are concerned with what is proper. You believe in punishment, when punishment is due. Once you give your word, it is a word of honor. You are a productive person who doesn't believe in loafing.

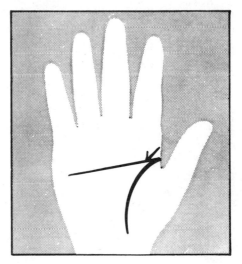

### -163-
### Your Head Line has a short inside fork at the onset.

You are given to frequent changes of mind without any good cause. You seldom know why you are so amazingly changeable. Fortunes and honors bestowed upon your parents will ultimately benefit you, but don't sit around and wait for them. You'll never know when they will turn up.

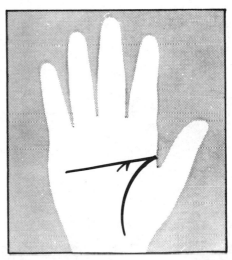

# HEAD LINE SEPARATED FROM LIFE LINE

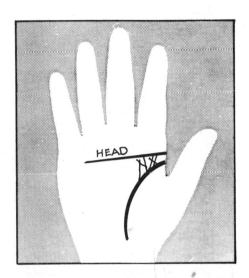

### -164-
### Your Head Line and Life Line do not merge, but are connected by branches and crosses.

You love all sorts of jokes. Without humor and a good hearty laugh every day, you feel life wouldn't be worth living. You like to play practical jokes. You are easily offended when the joke is on you, which is natural, because you are sensitive.

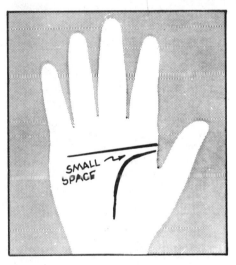

### -165-
### Your Head Line and Life Line are separated at the start by a very narrow space.

You are the active type with strong initiative. You fear no criticism. You are bold and daring, with enough wits to escape from real danger. You think independently and are able to make quick decisions. Along with your physical boldness, you possess a mental daring, which puts you one step ahead of your adversaries on all counts.

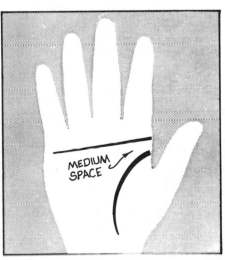

### -166-
### Your Head Line is separated from your Life Line by a medium-sized space.

From time to time you are lighthearted and let your fantasies run wild. And sometimes you let the tension of anger accumulate until you are a giant knot. This hostility can trigger other undesirable moods, like fear and sadness, which make you weary.

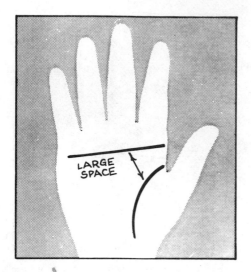

### -167-
### Your Head Line and Life Line are generously separated at their onset.

This is an indication of impulsive rashness. You have a bulldog obstinacy. Your restless nature can turn into recklessness. You do not proceed cautiously with those who feel tenderness for you. Sudden surges of energy and feelings make it difficult for you to make wise decisions.

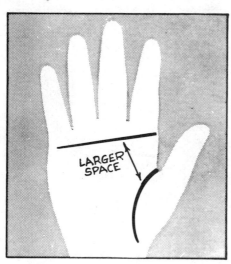

### -168-
### The distance between your Head Line and Life Line is excessively wide.

This is a sign of a frantic, passionate, and hasty nature. The muddles that give you infinite trouble can be cleared up by disciplined planning. Because sometimes you don't believe you have the strength inside to complete things started, you get discouraged. Your tenseness can cause a lack of confidence. You have an enormous inner reservoir of abilities which haven't been explored.

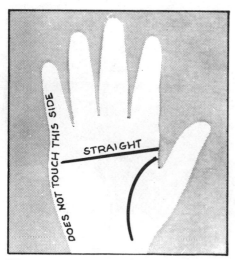

### -169-
### Your Head Line stretches straight across the palm and does not touch your Life Line.

You have an immense power over others. This skill would fully develop if you went into public life. You possess alacrity of thought, and attain in an instant what others struggle for. You, above all, must have a definite purpose in life. Without a goal, you are like a captainless ship drifting at sea.

### -170-
**Your Head Line is separated from the Life Line and moves towards the Mount of Mars.**

You are a self-appointed leader. You enjoy organizing gatherings. You would sacrifice everything (family, friends) for what you believed to be your public duty. You have discovered that the public consists of a mass of fools, and you are determined to do something about it.

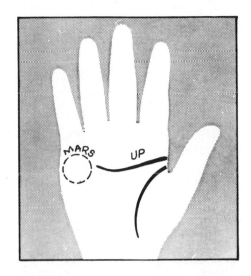

### -171-
**Your Head Line, separated from the Life Line, slopes downward towards the heel of the hand.**

You are inclined to work hard, only if you are in the right mood. If the mood doesn't strike you, you struggle and push yourself through tasks. You have inherited a brilliant imagination and often forget that LIFE means ACTION.

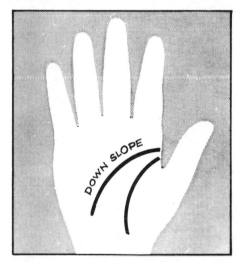

### -172-
**Your Head Line begins inside the Life Line and proceeds straight across the palm.**

You have a sensitive streak, and the slightest disturbance can sometimes trigger an unpredicted emotional outburst. Later in life, through an insight, you largely overcome this vulnerability. You feel wrongly treated, but your imagination makes it worse.

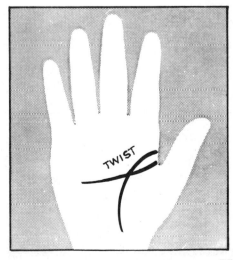

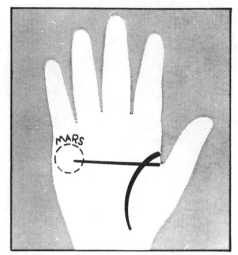

### -173-
**Your Head Line begins inside the Life Line and proceeds straight across the palm towards the Mount of Mars.**

This means you have the mental "Mars" quality. Through Mars you have the strength to fight for what you believe in, and you spring back unscathed after a defeat. You might feel weak, but Mars will always give you all the strength you need. Though you may feel timid and not up to facing challenges, Mars will also give you the courage to overcome most any weakness.

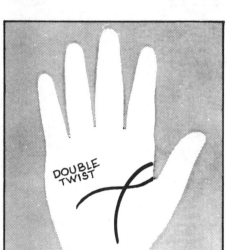

### -174-
**Your Head Line curves downward and has its origin inside the Life Line.**

This means you tend to be overly cautious. The result is that at times you carry yourself shyly. You withdraw to protect yourself, because inside you feel sensitive. You fly off the handle easily and are hasty to do things you later regret. You do not trust your own mind power, which is the natural antidote to your weakness.

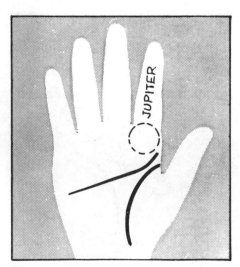

### -175-
**Your Head Line is not joined to the Life Line, but starts with a curve around the base of the Mount of Jupiter.**

You have been endowed with intelligence and a superior sense of reason. You hold yourself in high regard. Although your pride is justifiable, keep your mind open to practicing humility.

### -176-
### There is a cross-bar connecting your Head Line with your Heart Line.

Sentimentality and loving feelings are the forces that drive you onward. You devote a lot of your time doing for others. You have a giving soul. Beware of bestowing your generosity on the wrong people.

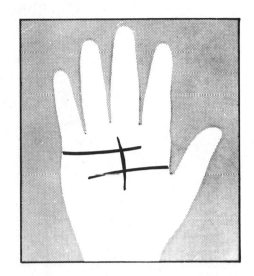

### -177-
### An upward branch of your Head Line leads into your Heart Line.

You have allowed coolness in matters of affection to slip into your romance. The cold logic that dominates in matters of love serves to protect your shattered feelings. Your Head Line gives you the mind to resolve this block through reasoning and thinking.

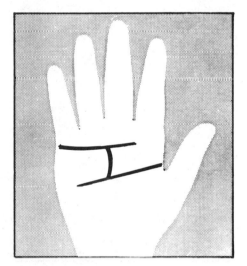

### -178-
### There is a small, even space between your Head Line and your Heart Line.

You could become more relaxed about living your life if you weren't so bitter about your losses. It is true that you have lost much and now are afraid of giving, as you feel you have so little left to give. If you could devise a way to stop repeating the losses in your mind and stop reliving them, you could open up a way to start receiving more.

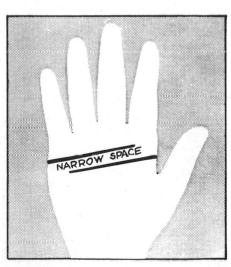

NARROW SPACE

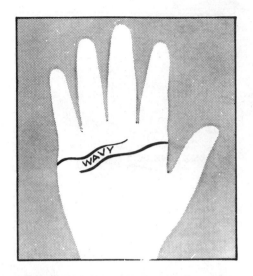

### -179-
### The space between your Head Line and Heart Line is narrow and uneven.

Without warning, your thoughts suddenly turn inward and focus on your pains and strains. You become overly concerned with your health and well-being. It is in these times that you become more sensitive to your surroundings. You feel more and you hurt more. In these times you lose your support from others and have no haven of safety.

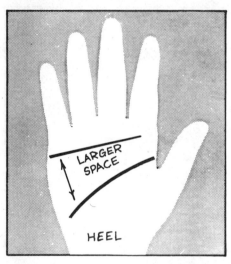

### -180-
### The space between your Heart Line and Head Line is generous, getting larger towards the heel of your hand.

This configuration signifies that as you grow older you become more grateful and more generous. Your dedication to others and the welfare of the needy becomes a major concern to you in your retirement years.

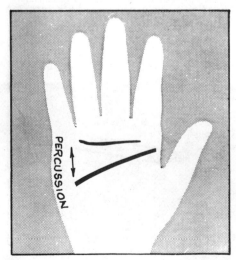

### -181-
### The space between your Head Line and Heart Line is broader on the Percussion side of your hand.

You have a healthy body and mind, and if you keep regular good habits, you will remain trouble-free in these realms. You believe in honesty and have a very low regard for liars. If someone lies to you just once, it's over forever.

### -182-
**The space between your Head Line and Heart Line widens towards the Mount of Jupiter.**

Others see you in a different light. You are not the conventional type. Stay proud of the very things that make you different, and don't give a hoot about what others may think of you. This way your genius and gifts have room to grow along with your confidence, as you stand before a great reputation and grand career through being different.

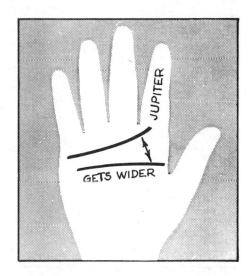

### -183-
**The space between your Head Line and Heart Line is a rectangle.**

You are blessed with an even disposition. This makes you a fair judge in crisis situations. You are also well-balanced in your bodily movements and would make a fair dancer or athlete. You are sure of yourself and you like to make your presence known wherever you go.

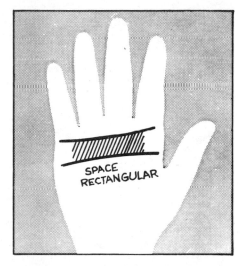

### -184-
**The space between your Head Line and Heart Line has broad and narrow areas, with the two lines coming very near each other midway across the palm.**

Depending upon your frame of mind, you can be either openhanded and loving or close-fisted and vengeful. In a flash your disposition can turn from cheer to churning. Both sides are very strong, and much of your time could be spent in making up with friends.

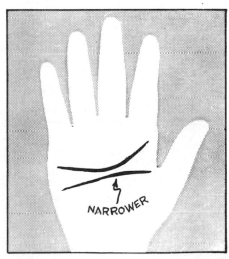

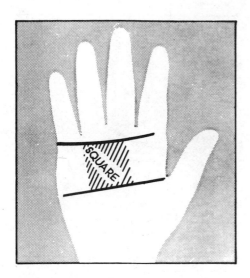

**-185-**
**The space between your Heart Line and Head Line presents an almost perfect quadrangle with equal width and length.**

You are strong-headed and resent being directed. You trust your instincts, not people. You always insist upon finding out all the facts for yourself. You are the born adventurer. You will go places that others fear most. Your attitude towards life is daring.

# HEART LINE

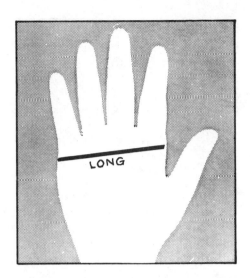

### -186-
### Your Heart Line is exceptionally long.

You have extraordinary depth of passion that you know how to cover up well. You can envision the maladies and suffering of others, almost as though you were suffering yourself. Your tenderheartedness attracts less fortunate persons in need of your support. You help them and must learn not to take their problems to bed with you at night.

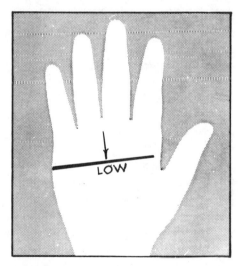

### -187-
### Your Heart Line appears low on the palm, almost touching the Head Line.

Your soft-heartedness makes you prey to panhandlers. You succeed when you learn to think your way through problems, much the same way as a scientist solves his. Avoid sharing your troubles with people, which is your weakness. Sometimes you allow disturbing sensations to grow so strong that they block out your logical thinking.

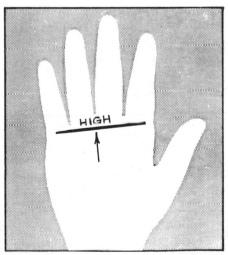

### -188-
### Your Heart Line is situated very high on the palm.

Affairs of the heart are ruled by strict caution. You vow to take no risks in love, and you calculate every move well in advance. Your mind is a probing, searching one, active and alert. With it you should be able to relinquish those old, worn-out negative thoughts for more realistic attitudes.

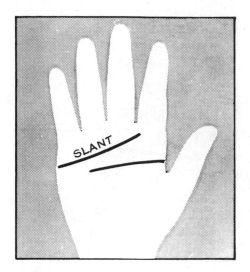

### -189-
### Your Heart Line slants towards the Head Line.

Mental powers have a strong hold over your feelings of the heart. When it comes to the choice between pursuing a romantic interlude or settling unfinished business, you run to the business. The battle between heart and reason (or profit) will go on until you learn the fine art of how to enjoy yourself.

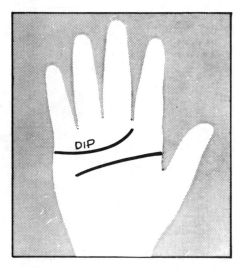

### -190-
### Your Heart Line dips towards your Life Line.

You have had the difficult task of overcoming some shocking and maturing early experiences. In some ways you can be grateful for them, as they make you better able to cope with the uncertain pace of life today. Your ideals change drastically as you grow older.

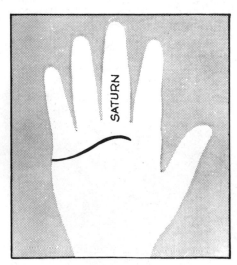

### -191-
### Your Heart Line deflects towards Saturn.

You are strongly drawn towards people of the Saturnian type. Saturnians possess a good deal of mature, sober qualities. These blowhards are good for you, because you are a dreamer. You need to learn from the Saturnians, who teach you accuracy and control. You will be fine, just as long as you do not pick up their pessimism.

### -192-
### Your Heart Line deflects towards Apollo.

Your heart is attracted towards the Apollonian type. These Apollonians have the power to lift your gloom. They are vigorous, healthy types who draw you into participation and action. They motivate you to shape an exciting life for yourself. You could call them the salt and pepper of your life.

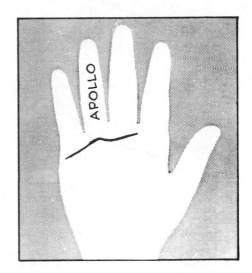

### -193-
### Your Heart Line deflects towards Mercury.

You have a strong attraction towards the Mercurial type of partner. Through them you satisfy your material needs and find security. Mercurians are shrewd, and usually rich in material assets. They are skilled with their hands and have tireless energy. You rely upon them to complement those parts of you that are not as strong.

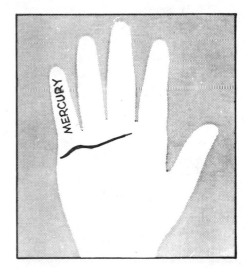

### -194-
### Your Heart Line extends over the Mount of Jupiter.

You choose your mate with only good intentions in mind. This sign signifies a lofty, pure, idealistic love—never love with ulterior motives. You can be a blind enthusiast with your love. You are so intoxicated with love, you wouldn't recognize a bad relationship.

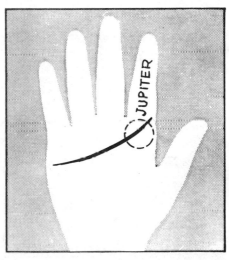

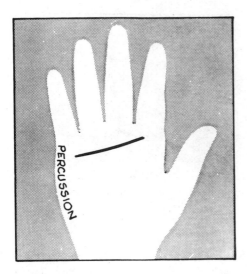

### -195-
### Your Heart Line goes across your hand right up to the Percussion.

You have an excess of affection. Sometimes your feelings of love and givingness are so overwhelming that there is not enough places in your environment for them to be appreciated. This causes a surge of frustration. You are often deeply hurt when your love is not justly returned.

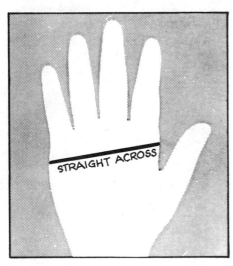

### -196-
### Your Heart Line stretches completely across your hand.

The length of this line reflects proportionately just how much love your heart embraces. The truth is, you have way too much heart. You allow sentiment to override your logic, and then you fail to protect your interests. Against your better judgment, you are inclined to loan money generously. You patronize out of sympathy. You show too much heart for your own good.

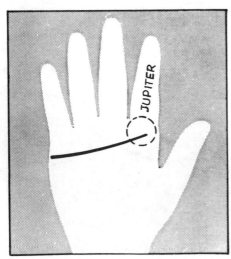

### -197-
### Your Heart Line starts on the Mount of Jupiter.

You have an unusually high code of honor. Your game of love is filled with rules that dare not be broken. You are most eager to have the people you love become rich and famous, and will dedicate yourself to this cause. You choose to marry your equal. Once you love, you love forever.

### -198-
### Your Heart Line begins between the index and middle finger.

You reflect the happy medium between idealism in love and the reality of sacrifice. You masterfully employ both to attain harmony in love. You are dependable in your affections, once you permit yourself to let go and love all the way. You work hard for personal satisfaction. On an intimate level with friends you show them your calm and deep nature.

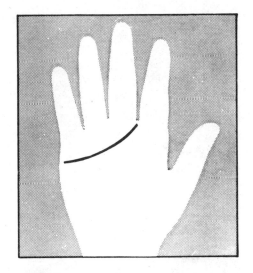

### X -199-
### Your Heart Line rises from the Mount of Saturn.

You are possessive about your friends and loved ones. You want them exclusively for yourself. If you discover any shortcomings in your partner, you are unforgiving. Sometimes when you err, you are not willing to admit it. You have the tendency to become bitter through disappointments.

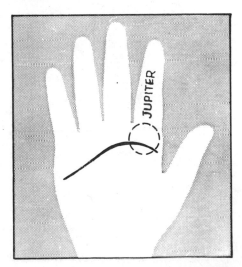

### -200-
### There is a downward curve in your Heart Line at the Mount of Jupiter.

You are wonderfully kind and affectionate. You are forever making up excuses for those who hurt you, justifying their actions. There isn't a mean bone in your body. For survival's sake in this world you should be firmer and more aggressive.

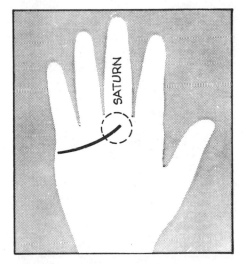

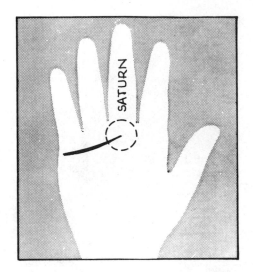

### -201-
### Your Heart Line rises under the base of Saturn.

You live more or less for yourself and are disconnected from those close to you. Once someone falls into your disfavor, they remain lasting enemies. You are what is called a "just so" person—everything has to be "just so," and no other way, or else you are extremely uncomfortable.

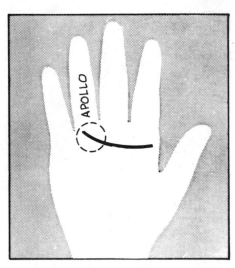

### -202-
### Your arched Heart Line terminates under Apollo.

This shows that down deep you are a true Apollonian, filled with ideas of art and beauty. You will be happiest married to an Apollonian, as they represent what you love most: playfulness, healthy robustness, vigor, geniality, and the sparkle of life. Your ideal love can be recognized at once as the partner who is fond of beauty and grace.

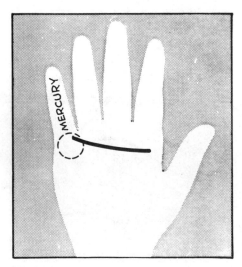

### -203-
### Your Heart Line ends high on the Mount of Mercury.

This shows that your affections are directly influenced by finances. You can't be happy unless you have money in your pocket. Mercurial shrewdness guides your heart. Love and money go hand in hand with you. You like to see yourself in fine clothing, and you are not averse to admiring yourself in mirrors.

### -204-
### Your Heart Line terminates on the Upper Mars.

You fall for the Martian-type person. These types embody the elements of aggression and force that you lack. They teach you to fight in business, to fight hard for the dollar. You learn from them to fight ferociously for love, as they do. These Martian-types awaken in you a feverish passion for all you long for in love. You fight to the bitter end to win the love you deserve.

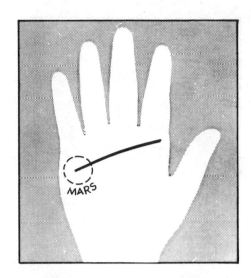

### -205-
### Your Heart Line rises under Jupiter and ends under Saturn.

You started out in life with the right sort of affections towards the opposite sex. Then your feelings went awry, and fear and dislike crept in. Your nature changed from hot to cold. You need a sunny, outgoing person to show they care for you. From them you need to be reassured and made to feel secure.

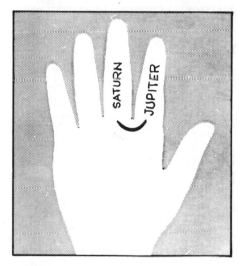

### -206-
### Your Heart Line does not run farther than the Apollo finger.

The length of this line tells you how much heart you have and how much you can give to others. Since this line is shaped normally but runs for only a short distance, it shows that you have run into serious difficulty, caused perhaps through loss and disappointment. You have made a decision not to waste your love on anyone.

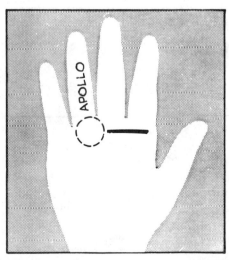

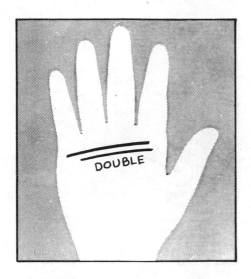

### -207-
### Parallel to your Heart Line runs a sister line.

This second line demonstrates extended devotion to a loved one or friend. You are loyal and faithful under most circumstances, and pride yourself in being able to keep secrets. You are the best friend a person could wish to have. When you love, you love forever. You are able to love two partners with equal intensity and devotion, or two partners are able to love you with the same fervor.

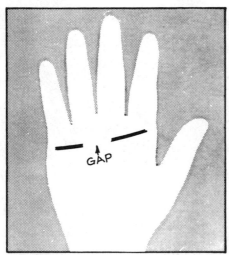

### -208-
### A broken Heart Line is evident.

The flow of love in your life has not always been even and steady. At times you feel you were unjustly robbed of love you deserved. You miss being loved consistently and continuously. Friends have also suddenly and without just cause broken off deep attachments. You sometimes feel contempt for others because of all these estrangements. As broken lines do mend with time, losses can be made up for.

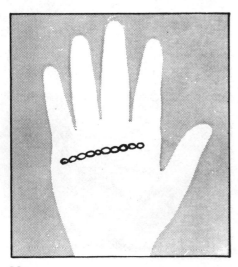

### -209-
### Your Heart Line is chained.

Your stability and routine is perpetually upset by petty intrigues. You permit others to meddle in your affairs and take control over you. Less and less do you value the worth of your own opinions. You try hard to please to win the love of people you need, but there are too many obstacles in your way. Gathering control over others will remove many obstacles.

### -210-
### There is a square covering an area of your Heart Line.

During phases of hardship and physical suffering, this sign of the square protects you from runaway calamity. The square provides comfort, eases the mind, and guides you to make the right decisions. The square could also be a stranger protecting you from an impending downfall.

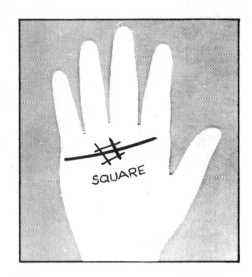

### -211-
### You have a very long Heart Line, with a clearly marked Girdle of Venus.

You harbor jealous feelings when the harmony between you and your mate is threatened. You can get physical during emotional outbursts. You lose your temper so suddenly, sometimes at the slightest provocation, that you don't leave any time to put a cap on these loose emotions.

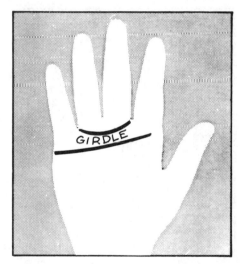

### -212-
### You have a weak Heart Line, with your Head Line separated from your Life Line.

You are very overprotective in your love relationships, afraid to lose hold of the threads that hold your relationships together. At times you deliberately court danger in love and are too eager to destroy what you have carefully built. You have excess nervous energy that could be channeled into refining your love relationships.

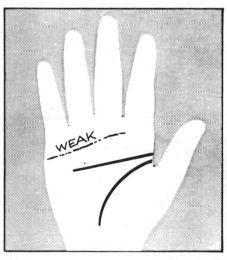

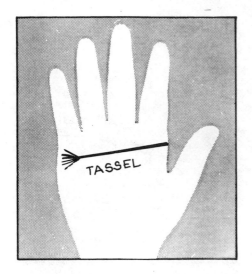

### -213-
### Your Heart Line ends in a kind of tassel.

For every little prong or branch of the tassel, a love affair of minor consequence has taken place. You have an affectionate disposition, with lots of love to spare, and are often blessed with a feeling of serenity and givingness towards humankind. Your kindliness and warmth are of the kind that holds marriages and families together.

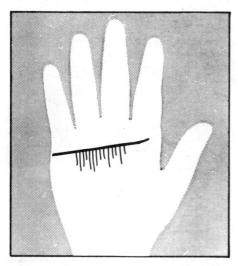

### -214-
### There are multiple fine lines dropping from the Heart Line into the area below it and above the Head Line—the Quadrangle.

You have always known that you are a complex, but versatile, individual. Sometimes you get frustrated, because you cannot put all your capableness into something that is worthwhile or moneymaking. You have aptitudes in a multiplicity of areas, and it might be hard for you to make a choice. You would be wise to concentrate on those activities that you do well, that bring you the greatest satisfaction.

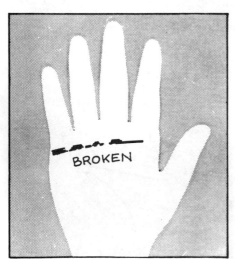

### -215-
### You have a Heart Line broken in many places.

There are parts of your personality that are marked by lack of constancy. You like to change friends and scenery frequently. You crave the newness and excitement that comes with frequent change. This might contribute to the feelings you might have that life is sometimes pointless.

### -216-
### Your Heart Line is broken under the Mount of Apollo.

Through a sudden, impulsive change of mind you break off a love affair of long standing. You feel superior to others, in part because you are a very capable person. This could grow into conceit. You were bought up in an arrogant atmosphere, which has somewhat rubbed off on you.

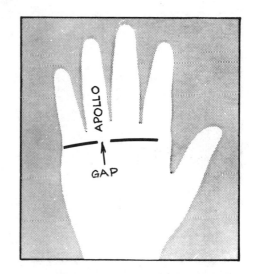

### -217-
### You have a broken Heart Line under Mercury.

Right now your thoughts are focused in on accumulating wealth. You could become a hoarder. You do not see yourself as stingy, where others do. Your love of money and security could go so far as to destroy bonds of love.

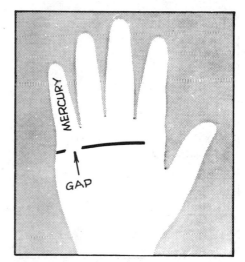

### -218-
### Two fragments of your Heart Line overlap each other.

You will be brought together again with a former love after years of separation. It will be a splendid reunion and a chance to begin a new, permanent relationship.

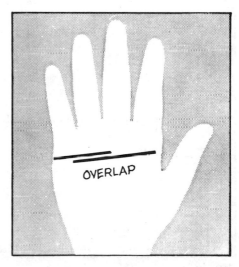

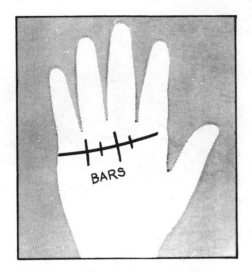

### -219-
### You have a number of bars cutting into your Heart Line.

Frustrations and unsettling conditions repeatedly show up in your love life. You wonder if you will ever come up from under these disappointments. Since the bars across your Heart Line are limited, your span of disappointments will also be limited.

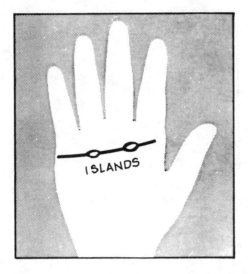

### -220-
### There are islands on your Heart Line.

You went through a number of episodes of desertion. These separations were through no fault of your own. Most likely you will not reconnect with old ties.

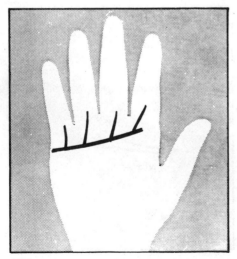

### -221-
### Your Heart Line sends branches upward towards the fingers.

These branches can be counted as the number of your successful friendships and close alliances. Those are the number of people who will see you through hard times and with whom you share a kindred spirit.

### -222-
### Your Heart Line casts a branch to the Mount of Jupiter.

The moderating influences of Jupiter bring honors and riches your way. This branch redirects your sex drive into services of personal enrichment. You are rewarded because of personal involvement and sacrifices in social issues.

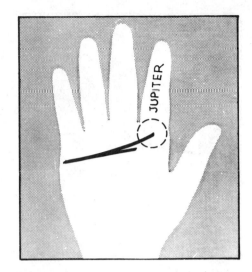

### -223-
### A line rises from your Heart Line and proceeds to the third finger.

A person offering much love and support fills your later years with warmth and comfort. Your mature years will be rich in joy and material rewards. It is then when you finally experience the meaning of true love.

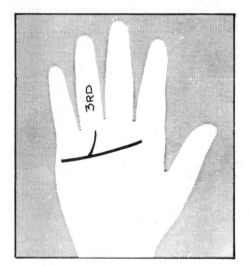

### -224-
### From your Heart Line springs an offshoot towards the Mount of Mercury.

Through perseverance, little by little, and starting very small, you amass a sizeable fortune. It is only your steady, untiring efforts that come to fruition. One who loves you deeply can accelerate your growth.

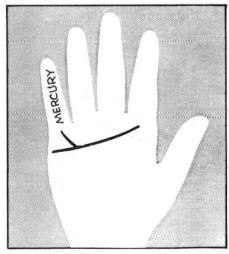

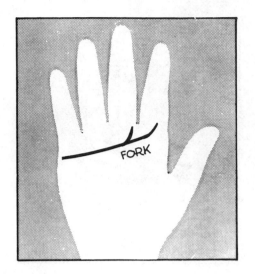

### -225-
### Your Heart Line is bifurcated at the start between the first and second fingers.

Your life turns tranquil after a period of sustained agitation. The ensuing peace makes you stable again. You have a well-balanced, happy disposition with lots of love to spare. You understand your partner's needs and feelings without any compulsion to change them. You know how to make compromises, never unreasonable demands.

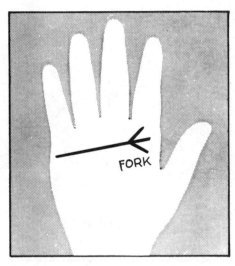

### -226-
### Your Heart Line begins with a three-pronged fork.

You are gifted with the spirit for justice. You have a strong inborn knowledge of the difference between right and wrong. This is perfect for services as a lawmaker or law enforcer. You are a dependable mediator in family affairs. Old and young alike rely upon your word.

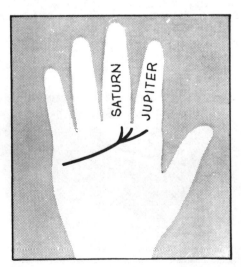

### -227-
### Your Heart Line rises and joins in a fork from three sources: Jupiter, Saturn, and in between.

Although passion is the driving force in your life, you learn the rules of common sense. You still have not learned the secret of how to enjoy yourself. You have love and affection to spare.

### -228-
**Your Heart Line is forked at the start, with one branch pointing towards Saturn and the other towards your Head Line.**

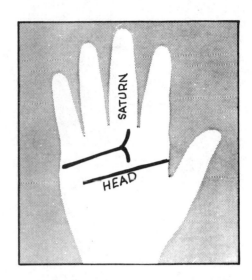

This indicates a spell of intrigue and departure from the norm in a location you do not choose to be in. Despite all deceptions and losses, you can pull yourself to greater heights. You are an easy mark for deceivers and cheaters.

### -229-
**Your Heart Line is forked under Saturn.**

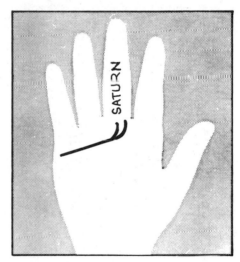

This is a very fortunate sign to have. With it you can fearlessly face anything involving danger or risk. You have the tendency to deviate from the conventional ways of doing things. There is a tremendous amount of energy behind your courage.

### -230-
**Your Head and Heart Lines are both forked at the start.**

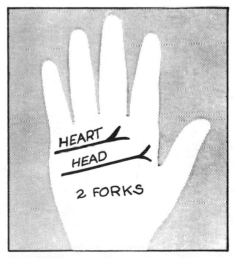

You will separate from your life's mate for a time. This is the period in which you will make enormous strides and mature in your interests. When the time comes to reunite, the union will be refreshing and exciting with your newly gained perspectives.

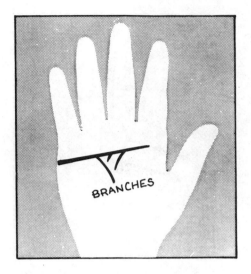

### -231-
### Your Heart Line bears downward branches.

These branches mark your past disappointments in love. Fortunately these lines disappear with time, along with the painful memories they represent. Healing comes quickest when you replace your losses with meaningful activities and pastimes that bring you immediate rewards.

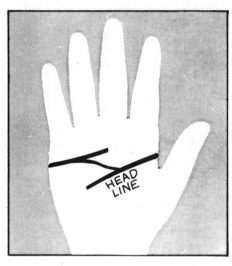

### -232-
### A line splits away from your Heart Line and gradually falls into the Head Line.

This shows that your feelings of heart have surrendered to your reason. An irritation or worry has caused you to be very careful in weighing the portions of love you dole out. Your love, now guided by reason and common sense, was once natural and flowing. You limit your chances of finding someone right for you by a barrier of criticism, which does not serve you well.

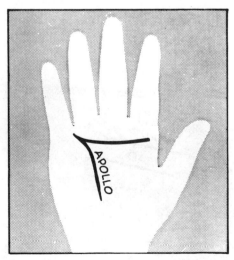

### -233-
### Your Heart Line merges into a rising Line of Apollo.

You may rise to a position of power, prestige, and wealth through an association ruled by affection. After you rise, others will greatly admire your splendorous lifestyle, and even use you as a role model.

### -234-
### Your Heart Line merges with your Head Line.

Losing your Heart Line to your Head Line shows that your affection for a specific person has disappeared and been replaced by a cool, distant, vacant feeling. Your feelings are now tinged with hurt and aggression. There are times of big trouble when you let anger rule you. Anger could destroy you, and it is necessary for you to calm your nerves in any way that works for you.

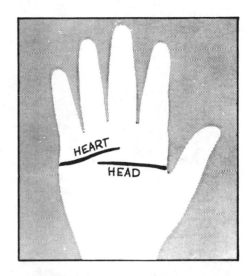

### -235-
### Branches from the Line of Fate, ascending to the Heart Line, branch off either to the right or to the left of your Fate Line.

Although you deeply crave an intimate union with the opposite sex, you fear the accompanying commitments and formalities. It is indicated that you enter several love affairs which do not end in marriage.

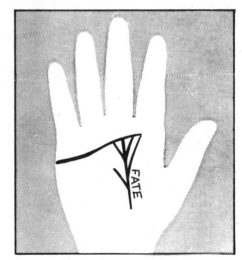

### -236-
### There are secondary lines connecting your Heart and Life Lines.

You have been defeated and disappointed in love on numerous occasions—too numerous to count. You have been the pursuer, the one who loved stronger, the one in love. You have always been the beseecher of your lovers. This lack of reciprocation could make you despondent or even physically ill.

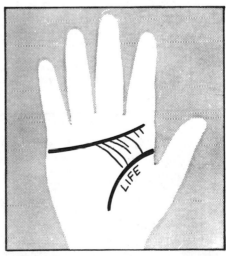

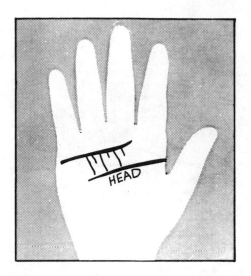

### -237-
### Lines from your Heart Line reach close to your Head Line without cutting it.

Your life is centered around the opposite sex. The opposite sex have the power to corrupt your thinking and manipulate you for their personal gain. Your greatness is not appreciated, because you have not learned the tools of self-assertiveness.

# SATURN LINE

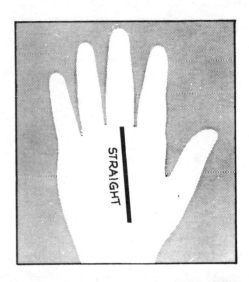

### -238-
### Your Saturn Line is straight.

This betokens happiness in old age. You become a part of a team that invents new things. You prefer to live in organized surroundings and feel uncomfortable in the overgrown, unruly outdoors. You have an inclination towards architecture.

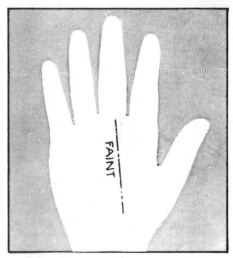

### -239-
### Your Saturn Line is hardly visible.

You are not fully convinced that you have a fate or destiny that is somehow connected to a divine plan. This line is usually absent in the hands of materialistically minded people. The fine details of your destiny are difficult to foretell because of your strong inclination to take life into your own hands.

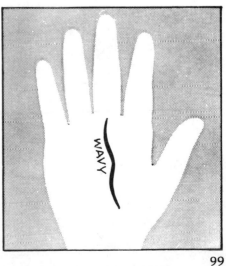

### -240-
### Your Saturn Line is wavy.

You are following a constantly changing course. You are led into situations you prefer to avoid. You let bossy people push their way into your life. You are exerting great efforts just to stay afloat. Don't rely on chance or any lucky numbers. Continue to force your way against the current that is compelling you—keep demanding your rights as a person and you will get there.

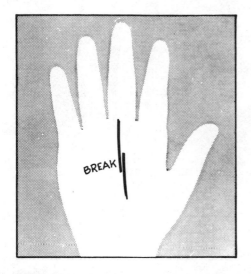

### -241-
### Your Saturn Line is marked with a single break.

After prolonged deliberation you initiate a major breakthrough. A change in your surroundings results. Change is brought about because you are "fed up" with your present situation. Your deep dissatisfaction spurs you to do the things you feared most. You find you are up to the challenge. Once the decision to change is made, you rise to the occasion.

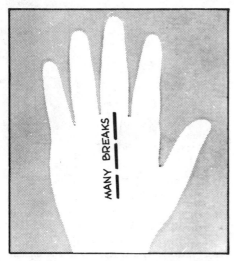

### -242-
### Your Line of Saturn has multiple breaks in it.

It is an indication that your happy moments tend to come in fits and starts, leaving you with intervals of loneliness and emptiness that are hard to bear. You are afraid now to go out and do the things you enjoy most. You are urged to make new and lasting friends.

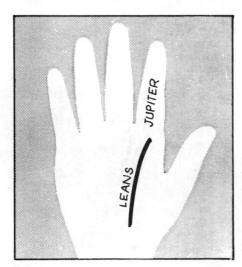

### -243-
### Your Saturn Line leans towards Jupiter.

Reward arrives after years of hard and often contemptible work. Material rewards depend largely on a factor of honesty. Someone might be waiting for you to rectify past mistakes. Patch up old misunderstandings and your work will be easier.

### -244-
### Your Saturn Line leans towards Apollo.

You take longer for breakthrough to happiness. There is an involvement in the arts that brings success. An unexpected arrival of riches in the family also brings added relief.

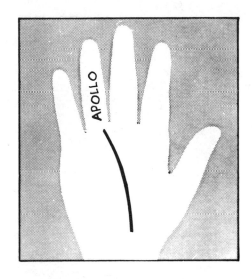

### -245-
### Your Saturn Line leans towards Mercury.

Sudden success in the field of business will come. By speaking up for what is yours and for what is right, others change their opinions of you. They begin to favor your company. You understand the ways of nature. This, combined with a flair for business, could be lucrative.

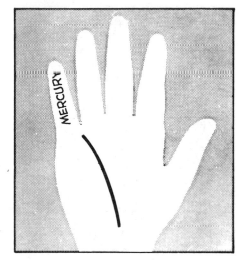

### -246-
### Your Fate Line terminates on the Mount of Jupiter.

You have an extraordinary destiny of only a chosen few. You enter a rare relationship. You dazzle everyone with your teamwork. Your whole life begins to center around activities that are shared together. It is also possible that you enter an equally bright marriage with your teammate.

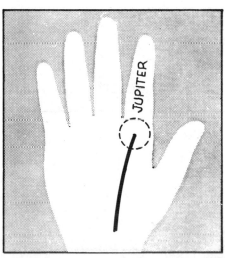

101

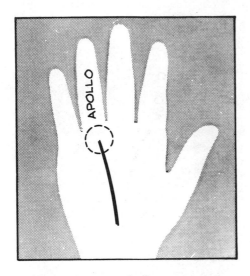

### -247-
### Your Fate Line stops on the Mount of Apollo.

Such an endpoint may be interpreted as an inborn love for the fine arts. You are the born collector of costly artifacts. And you enjoy being surrounded by the beauty of them. People with this line tend to devote their whole lives to cultivating their literary or artistic abilities. You wish to make your mark in your chosen field.

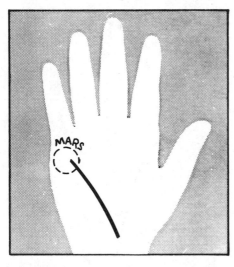

### -248-
### Your Saturn Line ends on Upper Mars.

You do not give up easily. You tenaciously hold on to your ideals. This power of resistance helps you to achieve success in leadership. You are a fighter and always know how to lift yourself up from discouragement.

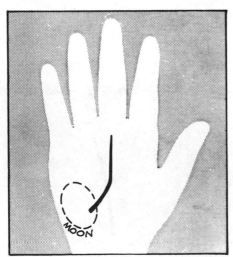

### -249-
### Your Saturn Line sets out from the Mount of the Moon.

There is a kaleidoscopic changing of events in your life that keeps you jumping. You have a tendency to let others push you around in your willingness to please and need for their approval. Until your life stabilizes, try to think of yourself first.

### -250-
### Your Saturn Line rises from the Mount of the Moon and runs to the Mount of Jupiter.

Your sign is a money sign. You are ambitious but don't always know quite how to do it alone. You lean on someone of the opposite sex. You believe that through their influence and guidance you will become prosperous.

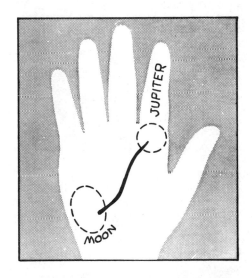

### -251-
### Your Fate Line begins from the Mount of the Moon and extends to the Mount of Saturn.

This indicates a unique destiny. Favorable qualities about you attract the public eye. Either in the field of politics, entertainment or in the arts, your star is sure to shine. You know how to stimulate the imagination of others.

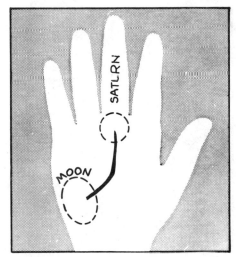

### -252-
### Your Saturn Line rises from the wrist and extends towards your Saturn Finger.

Nature has given you all the prerequisites for a brilliant and successful life. Once you start in hot pursuit of your goal you will discover all of your hidden resources. Guard yourself from people who talk you out of your ideas and plans.

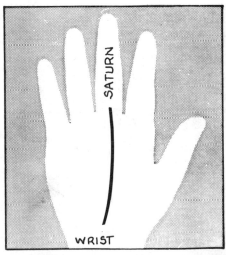

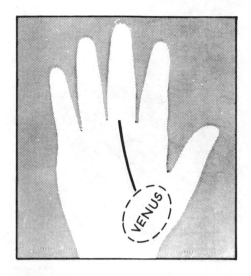

### -253-
### Your Fate Line rises near the Mount of Venus.

Your passionate love affects your whole career. In the past you have given affections to impossible people. Your ex-companions were pretenders, and you didn't have them all to yourself. You need to screen your friends more discriminately.

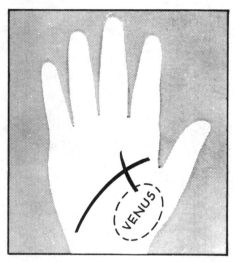

### -254-
### Your Fate Line starts on the Mount of Venus and en route crosses over your Life Line.

Your family plays a large role in influencing your life. You are indebted and grateful to them, but find yourself inextricably bound.

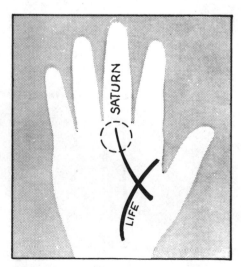

### -255-
### Your Saturn Line rises inside the Life Line and runs onto the Mount of Saturn.

This indicates that material success awaits you. Near relatives assist you greatly, because you convince them of your reliable talent. You have the energy and brains to do any job well.

### -256-
### Your Saturn Line is missing in the lower palm and begins its course in the Plane of Mars.

You have had an extended period of struggle coupled with financial uncertainty. All is not lost. As your trouble recedes you become organized as you once were and assets will begin to accumulate.

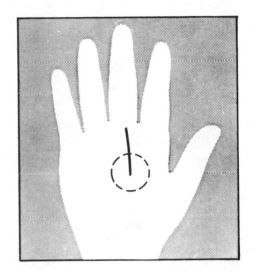

### -257-
### Your Saturn Line rises in the center of the the palm and runs into the Mount of Saturn.

You achieve success in life largely through your own efforts. You finally come to realize that your luckiness is nothing more than using your common sense and acting fast when the impulse strikes. You must apply yourself more than others and work on your powers of concentration.

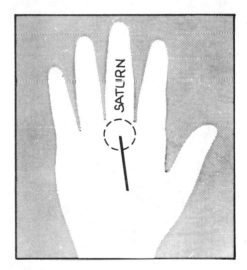

### -258-
### Your Fate Line begins in the center of the palm and leans towards Apollo.

This shortness of line indicates that you might have had a difficult childhood, or have had to struggle more than others to gain ends. Life has taught you many lessons. Your biggest asset is the understanding that you are the sole architect of your own fortune.

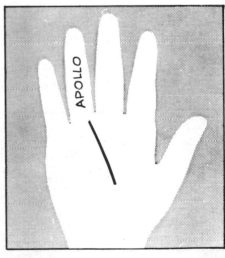

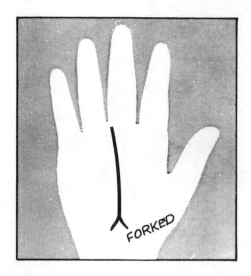

### -259-
### Your Fate Line starts with a fork low in your hand.

Your love of people prompts you to take outsiders into your family and under your wing. You accept people for what they are and do not try to project yourself into them. You do not fear strangers or strange situations.

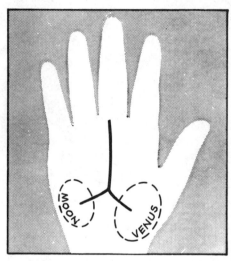

### -260-
### Your Saturn Line is forked quite widely at the start, with one prong into the Mount of Venus and the other into the Mount of Moon.

You put up a great struggle for success against great odds. The energy you need could be generated by some great love or inspiration of beauty. Don't let your imagination handicap you, as you are vulnerable to this.

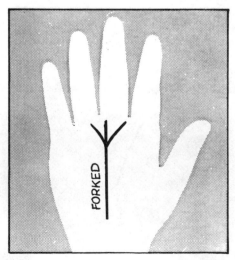

### -261-
### Your Saturn Line is forked at the end with two or more prongs.

One prong means ambition, two prudence, and three, brilliant intellect. These are your invaluable assets. Your dominant trait is your desire to succeed by winning the approval of others. You need not be afraid to exert yourself to the limit.

### -262-
### Your Saturn Line is clear and straight, ending with a single star on the Mount of Apollo.

You find yourself early in life. Because of this, your accomplishments will be celebrated. Later you will be sought after and popularly honored.

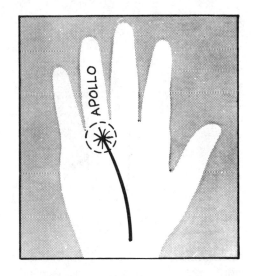

### -263-
### Your Line of Saturn intersects with a sloping Head Line.

You lean towards transactions that involve elements of risk. Playing with high stakes doesn't worry you. There is too little concern for the risks of loss. You also speculate in your love life, which puts you in hazardous predicaments.

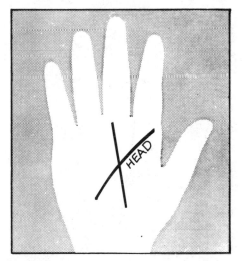

### -264-
### A portion of your Saturn Line sends off a branch to the Mount of Jupiter.

One higher-up takes notice of your leadership abilities. They offer you a giant step in your career. A new position fills you with will power and prestige. You must learn to carry a heavy load of responsibilities.

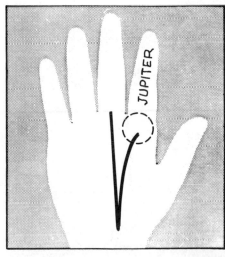

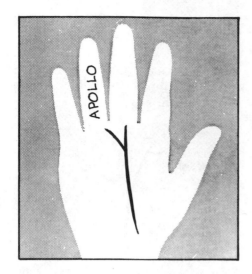

### -265-
### Your Saturn Line sends off a small branch which points to the base of the third finger.

This line is associated with exceptional command of the language or the pen. New channels of success could open for you while pursuing this direction. You deal well with the public. Public monies also pass through your hands. This is the palm line carried by many successful politicians.

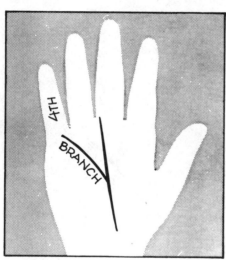

### -266-
### Your Saturn Line sends off a branch to the base of the fourth finger.

Your success is always obscured by your doubting nature. Your carefulness and suspicions limit your exposure to things, people, and events, which could bring you new opportunities. Your special achievements are in the fields of science or industry.

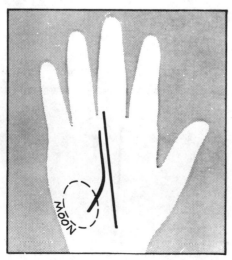

### -267-
### Your Saturn Line is running its normal course and is also supported by another line from the Mount of the Moon.

You enter a force-filled relationship with a member of the opposite sex. It is a strong union with permanent ties. A marriage to this energetic person will enrich you in every respect.

### -268-
**Your Saturn Line sends one branch to the Mount of Moon and another to the Mount of Venus.**

You have a tendency to let your passion and imagination conquer reason. Romance and passion dictate your actions and draw you away from professionalism. You are attracted to unreliable people. You dream of being first but are always last.

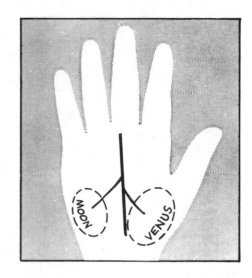

### -269-
**Your Saturn Line is straight and full of branches which rise upward.**

Change is in your gravitational field. Changes are always happening to you. Permanency is something you long for. In your lifetime you will know both poverty and riches.

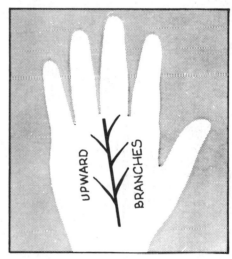

### -270-
**You have a Line of Influence coming from your Mount of Moon, which does not unite with your Saturn Line.**

This feature shows that at one time you let another gain dangerous influence over your life. You learn a tremendous lesson from this, which teaches you self-reliance. You become a person who lives life to the fullest.

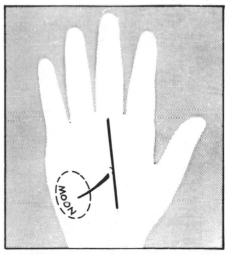

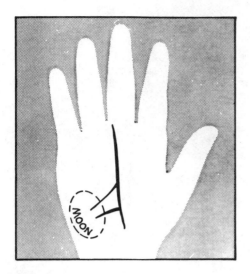

### -271-
### Your palm shows an Influence Line originating on the Mount of the Moon and ending in connection with your Saturn Line.

There has been much seething turmoil within you. When you reach the boiling point, you turn into a new person, like a caterpillar evolving into a butterfly. The new inner gleam within you will make you forget your past.

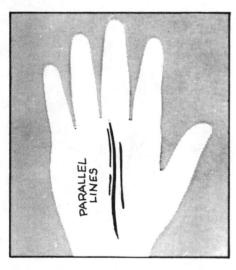

### -272-
### You have Chance Lines that do not touch the Saturn Line, but run alongside it.

These lines exert a strong influence on your career. You feel that your career is not progressing as fast as it could. Listen to close friends who are trying to guide you. They see your plight clearly and have an unselfish interest in you. You resist their suggestions because you are very proud.

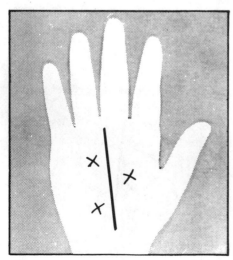

### -273-
### A cross exists alongside your Saturn Line.

Here the cross indicates a major change in life. You come to a crossing—a change in either jobs or homes. You have many dormant abilities that need awakening. Inner consolation comes after a resting period. Boredom is the enemy you fight all the time.

### -274-
**Lines from different Mounts are found simultaneously crossing your Line of Saturn.**

Factors beyond your control have slowed you down and brought your career advancement and lifestyle to a near standstill. You need to let everyone who counts know that you, too, have a voice.

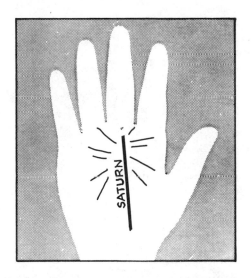

### -275-
**You have more than one Saturn Line, and they may point towards different Mounts.**

Your income eventually is derived from two different careers. You might end up practicing both careers at the same time—your principal career being your studied profession, and your secondary career being a former hobby or interest.

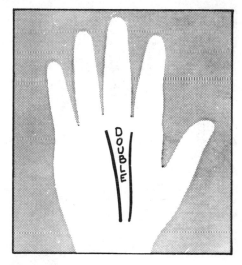

### -276-
**Your Saturn Line is intercepted by your Head Line.**

Until now you have been guided by others' expectations of you. The time is nearing when you no longer need to rely upon their encouragement and reinforcement. Your own ideas are very strong now, and you must develop your own emotional first aid.

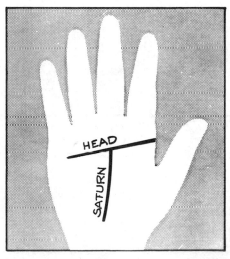

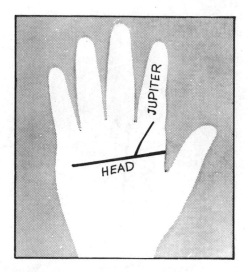

### -277-
**Your Saturn Line starts at the Head Line and crosses over the Mount of Jupiter.**

You are extremely proud of having something that no one else has and are afraid of losing it. Fear of losing what you have earned arrests your progress. You do not feel as important as you are.

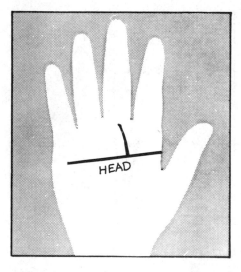

### -278-
**Your Saturn Line begins from the Head Line.**

Your clarity of thought and matureness shape your career in such a way that in middle years you find yourself in demand. If you stay active and always dare to test your strengths, you will look back at amazing accomplishments.

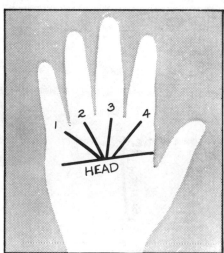

### -279-
**Your Saturn Line arises from the Head Line and travels upwards towards the fingers.**

Rewards for your steady efforts accumulate, and later in life they will arrive as a belated surprise. In the middle of your life you will regain your self-esteem, and this new dimension of pride will give you new energy to start new projects with full force.

### -280-
### A Chance Line from your Head Line runs alongside your Saturn Line.

You do not discourage easily. You are strongly driven to get over all your difficulties by yourself. You think with a clear head. You are an impartial judge of persons and a keen observer of facts and details.

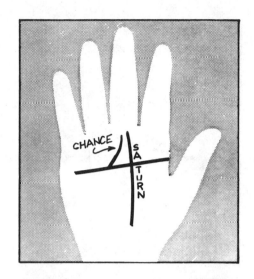

### -281-
### Your Saturn Line begins its course from the Life Line.

You are proud to exclaim that you are a self-made person. At times you feel unlucky and helpless and that life has done you wrong. These bumps and turns have set a pattern in your life. If you could free yourself from the past, you would gain control of your life again.

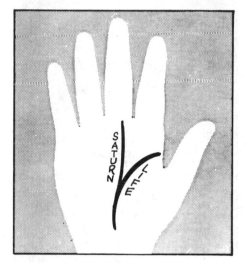

### -282-
### Your Saturn Line flows into your Heart Line.

This blend of lines is a prognosis for a happy and prosperous marriage. You make your marriage into a profession. You are attracted to your partner because of unusual ideals and caprices, which later try your patience. If you wait out the trying times, these growth pains will turn into something magnificent. Your partner awakens in you the adventure spirit.

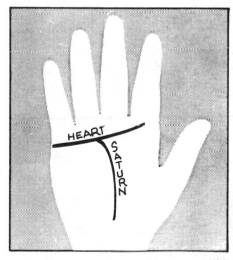

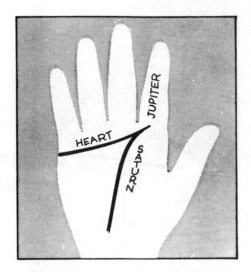

### -283-
### Your Saturn Line joins the Heart Line and ascends to the Mount of Jupiter.

Your nature is to be undemanding and overly affectionate towards those you love. Your caring nature spreads and repels love. Some admire you for this and others divorce themselves of you. You are the type who must give love. This combined with a profession could accomplish tremendous feats.

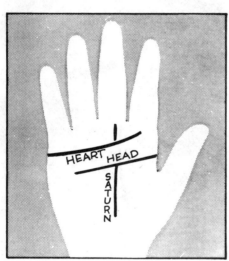

### -284-
### Your Saturn Line disappears between your Head and Heart Lines.

Projects that you have developed from scratch and poured your heart into have led to nowhere. These disappointments, maybe one after another, have deadened your motivation to start anything anew. There is a fatal flaw in common with all of your projects. Find your error in judgment, and there will never be a project again too large for you to handle.

# APOLLO LINE

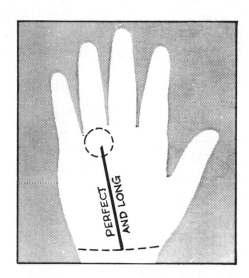

### -285-
**You have a flawless Apollo Line that starts at the wrist and runs straight towards the third finger.**

You were a gifted child and received special attention at an early age, which enabled you to gain a head start in your field of excellence. You soar to the top, leaving everything average behind. You like to challenge your mind, and solve difficult problems without assistance. Others are magnetized by you.

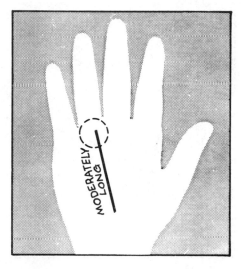

### -286-
**Your Apollo Line is clear and long and extends to the Mount of Apollo.**

This signifies knowledge, creativity, and love of the arts. Choose any of the realms of art, and you will receive recognition if you persevere. You may have to push yourself, as you do not always feel creative, but once you start going, there's no stopping you.

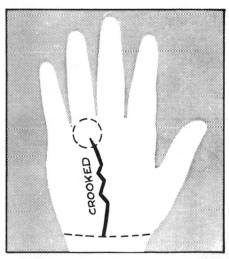

### -287-
**You have a slightly crooked line of Apollo which reaches from the wrist to the Mount of Apollo.**

You were born endowed with a great talent. Others take years to learn what you do naturally and without practice. This creative talent continues to develop unconsciously through observation and imitation throughout your entire life. Instant and enduring success is yours should you use this talent as a means to make a living.

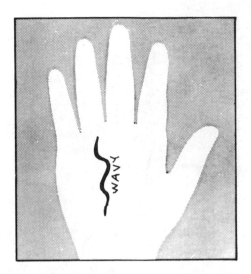

### -288-
### The path of your Apollo Line is wavy.

You have many gifts and talents. An unsteady application of discipline causes you to doubt your strengths. Take a serious look at the use of your time. See if wasteful hours are spent postponing success. You sometimes are made to feel like an outsider.

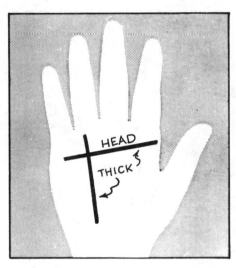

### -289-
### Your Head Line and Apollo Line are both straight and thick.

This combination gives you a drive to absorb yourself in the accumulation of material things. You never settle for mediocrity. You work steadily to fuel your blazing ambition to be the biggest success imaginable. You amass a fortune, not by chance, but as a result of good planning.

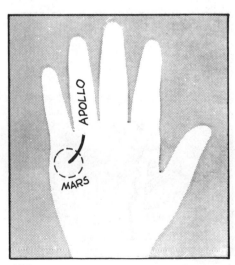

### -290-
### Your Apollo Line is rooted in the Mount of Mars and moves towards the Apollo Finger.

This line maps out success on a project that has already cost many years of labor and frustration. Most don't realize the number of obstacles you have had to overcome to be where you are today. You would like to abandon the present project because of frustration.

### -291-
### Your Apollo Line is rooted in the Mount of the Moon and moves towards the Apollo Finger.

You involve yourself in the lives of others. You are frustrated because people in your surroundings change their plans continuously. When you do not clearly understand the motives of others, you get confused and angry. Much of your success depends upon the cooperation of others.

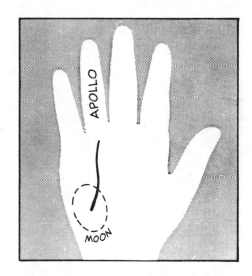

### -292-
### Your Apollo Line begins at the Mount of the Moon and points towards the base of the third finger.

Your strongest asset is your manipulative power over others. You magnetize people to sway them your way. You can change people's emotions with the flick of a switch. A friend of yours will serve as your mentor and bring you one step forward in your career. Others are intrigued by your manner of speech.

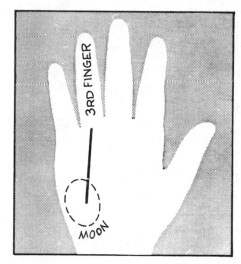

### -293-
### Your Line of Apollo begins low and runs only a short distance.

In your childhood you relied on your natural creative talents to outshine others. Since then you've gotten sidetracked and have dropped interest in the gifts God gave you. Something is holding you back from picking up where you left off.

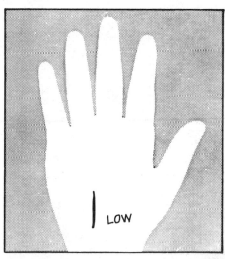

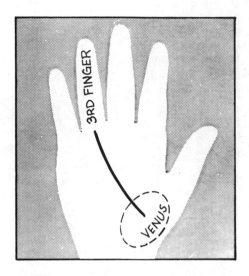

**-294-**
**Your Apollo Line originates on the Mount of Venus within the Life Line and projects towards the third finger.**

You have the facility for learning quickly and remembering figurative details. At the onset of your career, family members help you. You visualize with ease and have an excellent memory for visual details. You can accomplish outstanding feats with this gift.

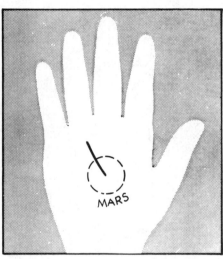

**-295-**
**Your Apollo Line begins on the Plane of Mars.**

This formation is associated with a long struggle for success. Because of setbacks and mistakes, others take to belittling you. You are brainy and consider life your university, as you strive to learn everything possible about life.

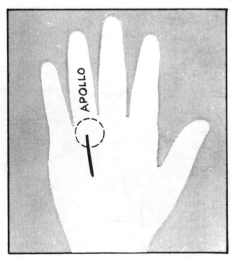

**-296-**
**Your Apollo Line rises high on your palm and runs onto the Mount of Apollo.**

You are the spontaneous type, full of play and cheer. You are a good judge of what is beautiful and artistic. You are more concerned with the beauty in dress, building interiors, and designs.

### -297-
**Your Apollo Line begins in between the Head Line and Heart Line and curves upward towards the third finger.**

You are the type of person who never takes "no" for an answer. You achieve success by way of dogged persistence. You are ready at all moments to find errors and loopholes. You like to outsmart others.

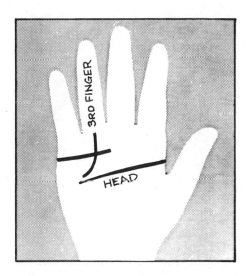

### -298-
**Your Line of Apollo rises high in your palm and covers the space between the Head and Heart Lines.**

During your formative years, a brilliant talent and sharpness helped you to glide past critical periods with ease. This special talent can help you again glide past present obstacles.

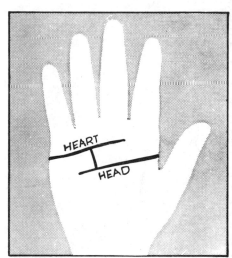

### -299-
**Your Head Line slopes downward. Its presence influences the direction of your Apollo Line.**

You overexert yourself at work trying to get ahead careerwise. You volunteer added work and this goes unnoticed. The more you do, the less you are appreciated. Find that contact person who will be the anchor of your success. Someone will have to open a channel for you.

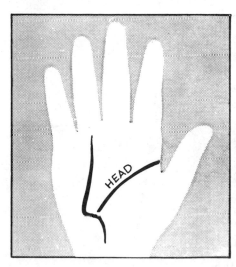

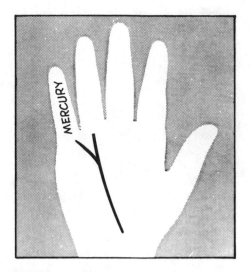

### -300-
### There is a fork at the end of your Apollo Line with one prong pointing towards Mercury.

Your talents are split in two directions. This diversity of interests robs you of valuable time to concentrate your effectiveness. Concentrate on your strongest talent. If you feel both are of equal strength, choose the one that is a realistic service and contribution to humankind.

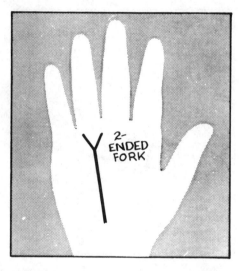

### -301-
### Your Apollo Line is forked at the finger end into two prongs of equal length.

As talented as you are, you are still waiting around for the actual results. There are several areas in which you excel equally well, and to which you are equally partial. But you cannot afford to divide your efforts. You might end up making an arbitrary decision choosing from one of your many talents.

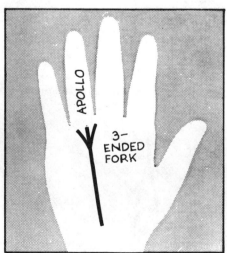

### -302-
### Your Apollo Line is divided into three forks at the finger end, and the forks rest under the Apollo finger.

You have unrealistic dreams of becoming famous. Deep down you are frustrated because many of the possibilities that passed your way somehow were spoiled. You weaken at critical moments. Think of your weakness as only an illusion, because that's what it is.

### -303-
### Your Apollo Line ends in three even branches.

There is some evidence that you spend more time imagining your success than planning for it. You need to work out a plan to improve your efficiency, to make your own personal blueprint for success. Then you will surprise others by accomplishing your goal in record time.

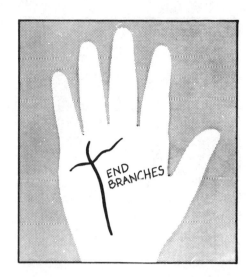

### -304-
### A short bar crosses your Apollo Line.

Harmony is the most important factor for furthering your career. This includes harmony at home and at work. Persons closely allied to you become angry with your stance of self-defense. Others expect you to sacrifice your pride for the sake of good will.

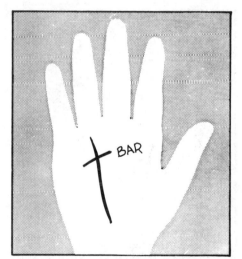

### -305-
### Your Apollo Line is accompanied by lines barring it up and down.

This implies that there are some major obstacles barring your progress. The obstacles are envy and disfavor on the side of those posing as your assistants. They cannot follow you because of your superior talents. You show your lack of patience. In return you are received with lack of respect.

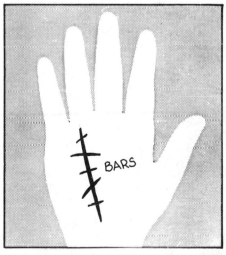

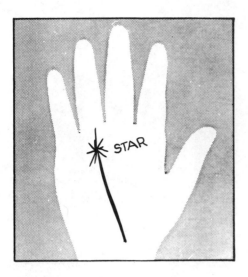

### -306-
### Your Apollo Line is carrying a star.

A star in this position intensifies your luckiness and positive magnetism over others. You have the power to sway the opinions of others. People with this marking have been known to change history. This is also the mark of the actor or vocalist, or a person with strong articulate attributes. Using this talent in a business venture could prove lucrative.

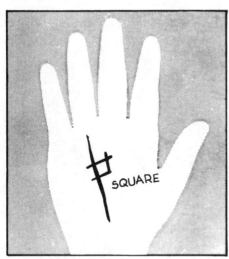

### -307-
### Your Apollo Line is marked by a vivid square.

You remain unharmed, despite vicious plots against you, however devious your assailants may be. The square signifies the guardian force that constantly guides you and cheers you onward. Through this you ward off treachery, enemies, and accidents.

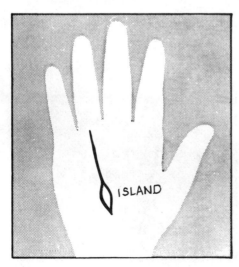

### -308-
### Your Apollo Line originates from a well-defined island formation.

With the right connections you are boosted into a career so startling that you become the envy of all who doubted you. An affair of the heart leaves you feeling empty and guilty. You feel you will never recover from this loss, no matter how you divert your attentions. You wound easily and are troubled because that love you want more than anything in the world seems so far off.

### -309-
### There are breaks and repair lines in your Line of Apollo.

You feel you have lost your motivation, or that the inspiration has gone out of your life. Things are not as they seem. Your enthusiasm is overshadowed by problems. Physical and mental activity will get your mind off these dark spots and bring you back into the swing of things. You need to search to find those things which excite you and inspire you.

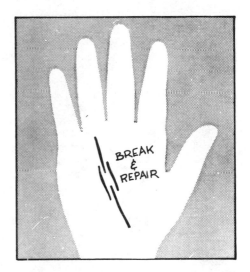

### -310-
### Your Apollo Line has three main branches pointing in an upward direction.

Each branch stands separately for an impulse during your lifetime to rise above average. You have a deeply rooted yearning to outshine others with a spectacular demonstration, which is backed by dreams of riches. You will be given three tremendously lucky breaks in your lifetime.

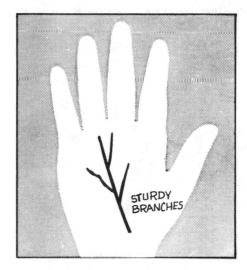

### -311-
### Branches of thin, fine lines rise from your Apollo Line and point upward towards the fingers.

You worry about not receiving the recognition of success due you for past achievements. Your greatest obstacle is worry about failure. Battling with this worry blocks your channels of success.

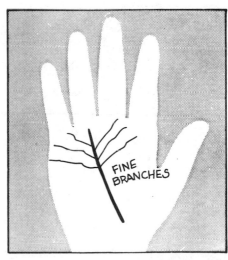

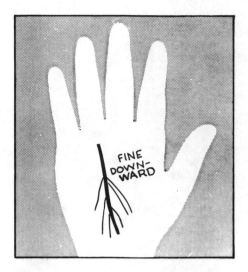

### -312-
### Fine lines fall from your Apollo Line and drop in a downward direction towards your wrist.

Each year you put forth greater and greater energies to come closer to your goal, and you feel you just aren't reaping a just reward. Sometimes you feel like you are pushing against a locked door. You hold the key in your own hand. Have an outsider analyze the problem. It might be related to poor work habits.

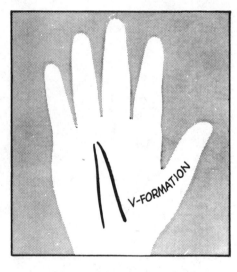

### -313-
### You have two Lines of Apollo set in a V-formation.

There are two forces tearing you in different directions. Serve the master who treats you fairly—the one who acknowledges you and praises you. Results come after a decision to follow your own thoughts and not another's. Once you follow one path, your dormant powers will give you enormous inner strength.

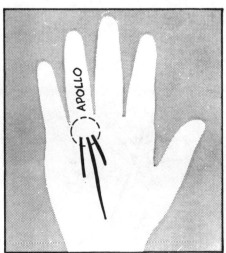

### -314-
### Several Lines of Apollo of unequal length rise to your Mount of Apollo.

You have a discerning eye and know what is considered excellent taste. The mechanics and techniques of various forms of art come easily to you. A diffraction of interests could delay your success.

### -315-
### Lines of equal length ascend to your Apollo finger.

This sign indicates great recognition through use of a talent. You rise not once, but many times to great heights. You may revive in spurts after your first rise to fame, and after that your success could reach a plateau. You retain your zest for life and try untiringly to improve upon your weaknesses.

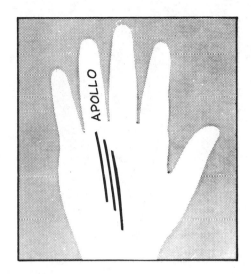

### -316-
### You have multiple Lines of Apollo, each of random length.

You must make a difficult decision to choose one of the many lines of work that are mapped out for you. Difficulty in deciding may lead you to choose that which is most interesting. You are cut out to do many things simultaneously, including running many businesses. The key to your success is to maintain personal supervision over all interests.

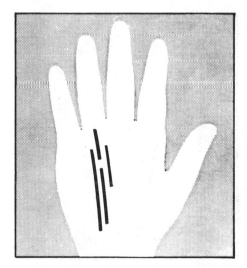

### -317-
### There are many vertical lines at the end of your Apollo Line.

You have a smattering of talent in several different fields. You are particularly intent on studying the diverse cultures of the world. To specialize in one talent, you must funnel all your energies into this one field, as you are inclined to scatter your vigor.

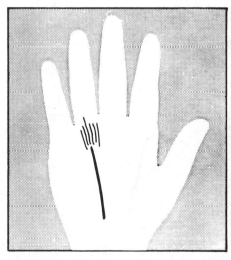

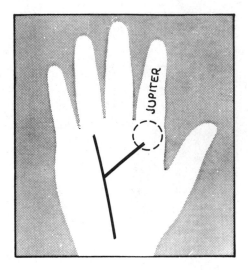

### -318-
### A branch leaves your Apollo Line and runs to the Mount of Jupiter.

Your ambition, coupled with great talent, drives you to feats of bewildering endurance. Once your mind is set on a goal, all your life's energies are channeled to achieve success. Others sense your leadership abilities and you feel comfortable in a dominant role.

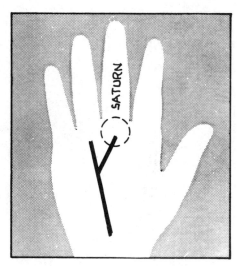

### X -319-
### A branch from your Apollo Line rises to the Mount of Saturn.

You are not led by tradition. You are strong-minded. With uncanny certainty you make yourself heard. Your glowing personality attracts the right people, who supply the right connections. You are a fusion of the two planetary combinations, Saturn plus Apollo. Saturn gives you sober frugality and fatalism; Apollo amplifies your liveliness and good humor.

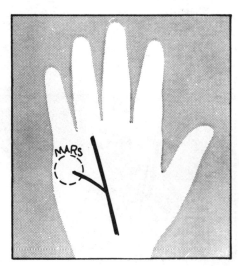

### -320-
### A branch from your Apollo Line rises to the Mount of Mars.

Added to your Apollonian character of vivacity and good humor is the power of Mars. The planet Mars imbues you with a fighting, determined, and resistant temperament. You should be able to stand alone and make your own way in life without any crutches.

### -321-
### A branch from the Mount of the Moon joins your Apollo Line.

Your future is closely linked to your ability to paint pictures in words. Whatever your profession may be, if you develop your power of verbal expression you will be on top. You would do well as an author or a music composer.

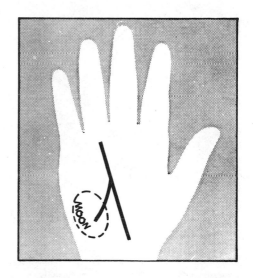

### -322-
### Your Apollo Line is joined by an upward curving line from the Mount of Venus.

This mark indicates that family money will pass many hands, but will eventually come to you after a period of trial and testing. It is also a sign of money gained through labor and frustration.

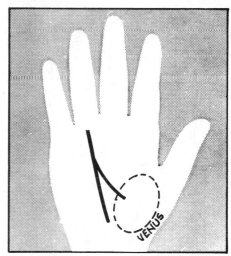

### -323-
### Influence Lines from the Mount of Venus run alongside the Line of Apollo.

This is interpreted as the intervention of relatives or close friends in the shaping of your career plans. Often this marking is read as a legacy. From relatives you receive counsel and financial support. They do assist you in time of need, but for a price.

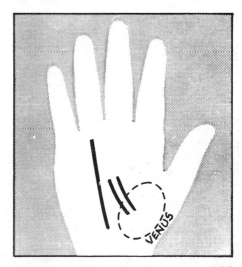

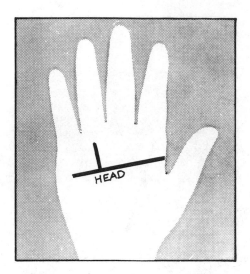

### -324-
### Your Apollo Line stems from your Head Line.

You are gifted with untiring determination to uphold the truth. You are prepared to postpone material rewards and sacrifice long hours and years of study for a small reward. You aim high, and thus need a profession into which you can put your heart and soul. Much of your toil and sweat will go unnoticed.

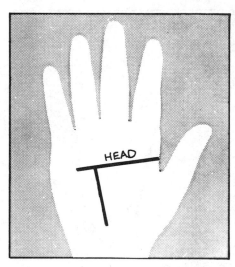

### -325-
### Your Apollo Line stops its course because of interference of the Head Line.

You have brilliant potentials, but are hindered in success because of a hidden handicap. In becoming conscious of your thought patterns and analyzing yourself, you overcome the handicap. Too much academic training or too much of an academic approach interferes with your artistic abilities.

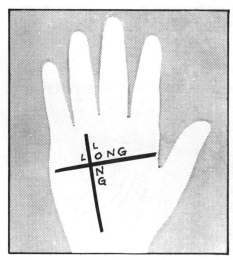

### -326-
### Both your Head Line and Apollo Line are exceedingly long.

You have quick mental reflexes and are willing to take big chances because you are sure of your planning, and therefore you make a prime candidate for big business. You feel sure of yourself, sometimes so strongly, that you could easily slip into high-risk speculations and even gambling.

### -327-
### Your Apollo Line has its origin in the Life Line.

You have the ability to turn menial chores into rewarding work. You are satisfied with your accomplishments. You are not ashamed to do hard work. You are proud of your heritage.

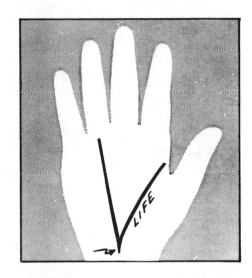

### -328-
### Your Apollo Line begins from your Heart Line.

There has been a delay in the arrival of material rewards for past efforts. In your golden years you will reap the success you are now working towards. Later in life you develop new ways to utilize your creative energy. In these middle years you learn compassion, love of beauty, and self-satisfaction.

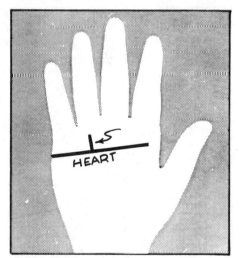

### -329-
### The course of your Apollo Line is stopped by your Heart Line.

Your potential to be outstanding and fulfilled cannot actualize to its fullest degree because of a blockage. This blockage is due to an absence of the right kind of love in your life. Once the giving has stopped in your life, your creativity and enthusiasm crumbles.

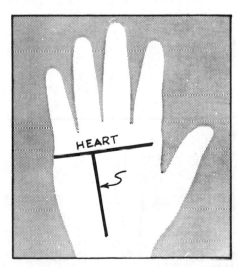

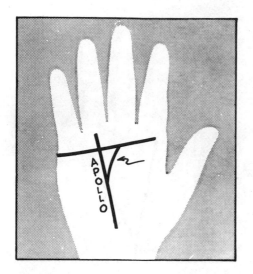

### -330-
### A line descending from your Heart Line merges with your Line of Apollo.

Many people recognize in you a frankness and wholesomeness. They reach out to you and want to be a part of this goodness. Also they will lend an arm and preserve your dignity in times of need. You blossom in the presence of others.

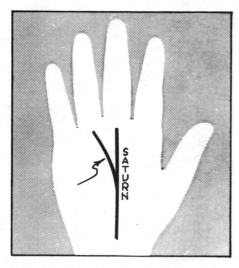

### -331-
### Your Apollo Line begins from the Saturn Line.

This is a line of distinction which predicts success in establishing a reputation of high standing. Your greatest chance of success is in a field that requires heightened sensitivity. Your only obstacle is some difficulty in handling the pressures and obligations of success.

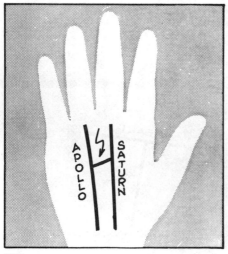

### -332-
### Your Apollo Line and Saturn Line are joined by a clear branch.

This can mean a legal partnership. It can also mean a marriage to a person with opposite interests, which works out well.

# MERCURY LINE

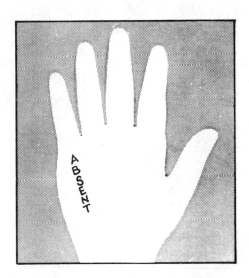

 **-333-**
## Your Line of Mercury is absent.

It is an excellent sign to be without this line altogether. Its absence denotes an extremely
robust constitution and a healthy state of mind.
A confident, trusting approach to life keeps
you in good physical and mental condition.

**-334-**
## Your Line of Mercury is curved.

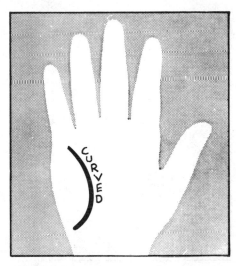

Nature gave you sturdy organs and a robust
constitution. Continued good health can be
yours, provided you do not abuse your body
with excesses. You have a high-strung and
sensitive temperament, with inspirations and
clairvoyance of a higher order. Some of your
clear, vivid dreams come to pass. Your type
inspires others.

**-335-**
## Your Line of Mercury is broken
## or discontinued.

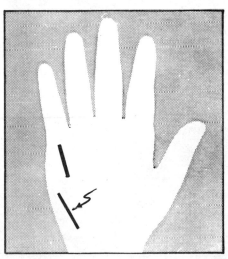

You do not have the power to resist temptations. Once your craving for something starts
you must satisfy yourself at all costs. Discipline doesn't work for you; your urges are
too strong. Others are waiting for you to weaken
so they can steal your place.

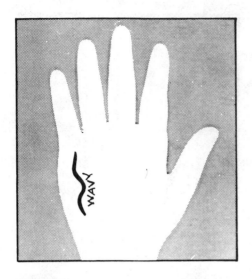

### -336-
### Your Mercury Line is wavy.

You are addicted to the wrong kinds of food, and the more you eat of them, the more you crave them. You especially crave the buttery, crispy, crunchy textures. It is very hard for you to find other projects that excite you more than food, but producing anything that makes you happy with yourself will divert your mind from the delicious.

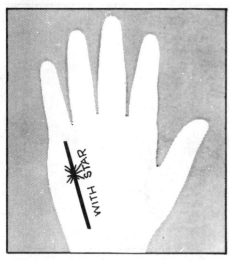

### -337-
### Your Mercury Line carries a star formation.

You are a many-faceted individual showing a scattering of great talent in many directions. If you are to truly succeed and find that one talent and put it to work for you, you will have to return to your earliest talent. You are the born professional-type because of your love of scrutiny and problem-solving. Once your confidence gets that little start and begins to grow, you do more than ever imagined.

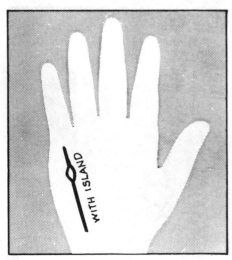

### -338-
### There is an island on your Line of Mercury.

An island closer to the wrist is the sign of a person who receives important clairvoyant messages through dreams. An island farther away from the wrist signifies that you will spring back from a bankrupt situation. This ruin will teach you the hard way everything you will need to know to become a permanent success the second time around. If this line has several islands in it, you will face repeated bankruptcies.

### -339-
### There are successive ladder-like bars aligned to form your Mercury Line.

Because of your stubbornness you hang on when others would have long given up the cause. You have a chronic problem in performance. In business, things could start going backwards for you. You have trouble pinpointing your problems. If a trouble-shooter told you what was wrong, it is doubtful that you would listen. A change in professions or businesses is in your favor.

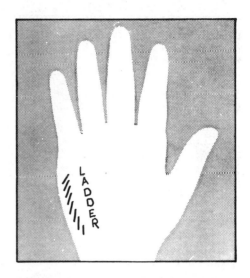

### -340-
### Your Mercury Line is interrupted by some spaces and gaps.

You have erratic work habits. You are distracted easily, and when you resume work, you find yourself on a different track altogether. It takes you longer than most to get a job done, and it rarely turns out to your satisfaction. You do not take too kindly to discipline.

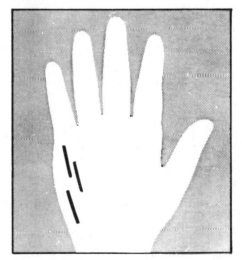

### -341-
### Your Mercury Line is formed of short wavy branches and curved broken lines.

You are not the easiest person in the world to please. You are ultra restless inside. If you could learn to use your fine-tuning, you would discover that you are picking up the discomforts and worries of other people. You have magnetic, psychic abilities, and instead of attracting contagious attitudes, you could throw off significant contributions.

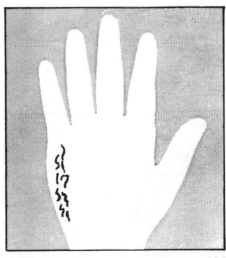

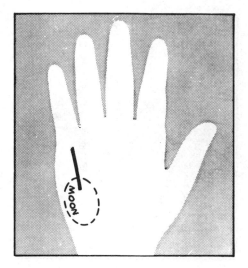

### -342-
### Your Mercury Line goes directly into the Mount of Mercury, avoiding the Mount of the Moon.

In your concern for a healthy old age, you aim at vigorous activity to keep fit. An aptitude for remembering a large number of facts is indicated. In your fantastic memory bank you also have stored many sorrowful events from the past. You compensate for losses by placing an inordinate amount of importance on money, because it makes you happier than most anything else.

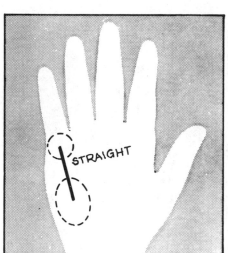

### -343-
### Your Line of Mercury is in perfect formation (starting at Mount of Moon towards Mercury).

Your assets are many: a strong sense of business, a spirit of discovery, vitality, a hopeful attitude, a merry disposition, a great sense of humor and wit, a stable nervous constitution . . . and on and on. Your strongest asset is your hypnotic power over others, which you may not have discovered yet. Your dramatic impact on people plus your hypnotic abilities might lead you into a successful career in politics.

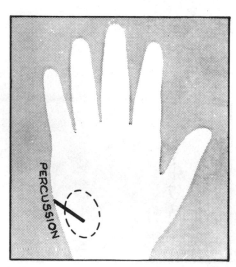

### -344-
### Your Line of Mercury is well developed with near-ideal outlines.

You think clearly and precisely, and are able to distinguish between fact and fantasy. Although your imagination is rich, you manage to keep both feet on the ground and concentrate on realistic, immediate goals. Dreams give you insight into things. You are strongly ruled by first impressions.

### -345-
### Your Line of Mercury is rooted in the upper area of the Mount of the Moon.

There are elements of truth behind your hunches and feelings. You are searching for the answer to a question that has been troubling you for years. You feel you have seen the answer many times, but are not able to recognize it.

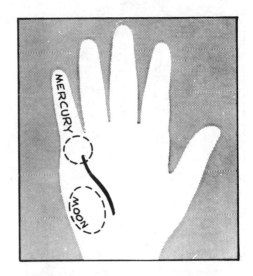

### -346-
### Your Mercury Line travels a straight course from the Mount of the Moon to the Mount of Mars.

This can signify that members of your family may also be your close friends or business partners. You are intense and fight for your freedom of expression. You are more serious than merry. You are the type who could become seriously involved in politics.

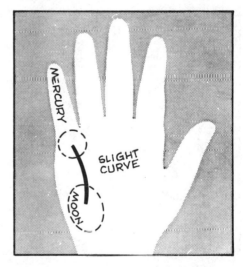

### -347-
### Your Mercury Line crosses the Mount of the Moon and leads to the Percussion of the hand.

Your character is as unpredictable and capricious as the sea. You know how to charm people using a kaleidoscope of moods and expressions, which change to suit the situation. You are full of mystery, and sometimes hardly understand yourself and why you do certain things.

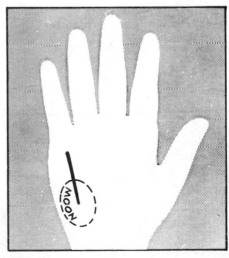

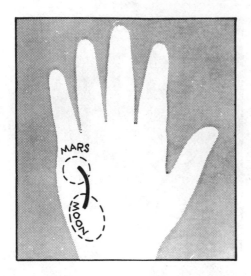

### -348-
### Your Line of Mercury begins on the Mount of the Moon and swings over to the Mount of Mars.

You are so good-natured that you aren't happy until everyone else around you is. When the chips are down, you surprise everyone with hope and cheer. You have persuasive ways about you, and you practice this in the interest of others.

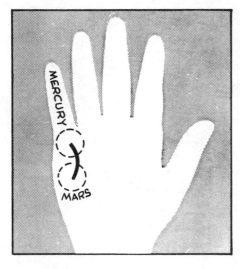

### -349-
### Your Mercury Line leaps from the Mount of Mars to the Mount of Mercury.

You are an emotionally triggered person with a lot of spit and wit. If you could keep a lid on your anger, your shrewdness could bring you far in business. You need enjoyable and constructive pastimes to soothe you and revive your vitality.

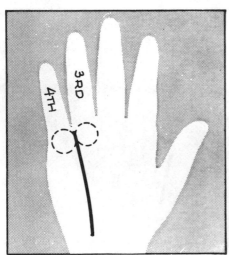

### -350-
### Your Line of Mercury is between the hills of your third and fourth fingers.

The direction of this line betokens a great reward coming your way as a result of a long, concentrated effort of superhuman endurance. You will suddenly be placed in the limelight, which will renew your spirit and strength. Your efforts will one day be noticed and appreciated by many.

### -351-
**Your Line of Mercury begins in the center of the hand and extends towards the Mount of Mercury.**

This signifies that you are thin-skinned. You are physically ambitious and have the vivacious personality that attracts admirers. You are alert and demand immediate satisfaction of your needs. You love to talk, and are an intriguing conversationalist.

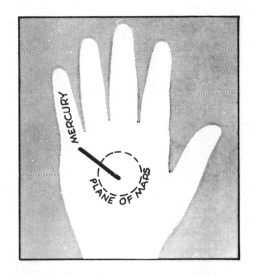

### -352-
**Your Mercury Line crosses the Plane of Mars (center of palm) in a winding fashion.**

Your perception of your physical discomforts is greatly exaggerated. That is, physically things are never as bad as they feel. You can maintain good health by including moderate outdoor activities in your daily routine. You are battened down in a rut, and it will take many years to develop a routine of outdoor physical activity.

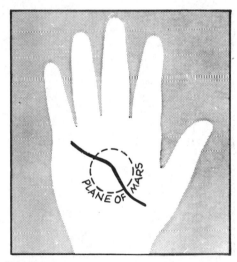

### -353-
**Your Line of Mercury crosses the Plane of Mars without any interruptions.**

This is a mark of a long life. At times you have exaggerated concerns for your health. You are a self-sufficient person. You like to get down to business. You are serious and direct.

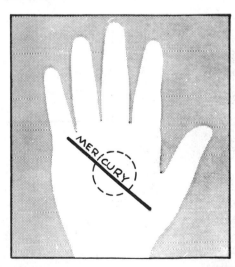

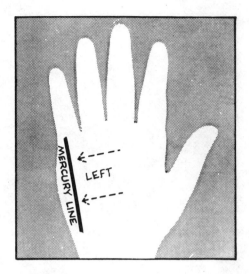

### -354-
### Your Line of Mercury is pushed over to the Percussion side of the hand.

You have a doubting disposition and because of this do not take full advantage of your clairvoyancy. You have not been at peace for a long time. Anger, frustration and rapid changes in your life have given rise to your restlessness.

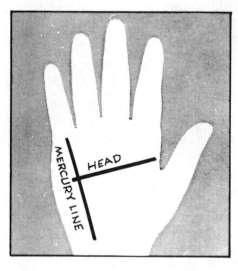

### -355-
### Your long, clear, straight Line of Mercury intersects with your long, straight Head Line.

The person with this mark should have an excellent memory. Since the Mercury Line is also called your Line of Liver, your diet and intake of fats could influence your mind and memory. If you want to sharpen your memory with this line, it is advised to cut out animal fats, sweetened processed foods and excess alcohol.

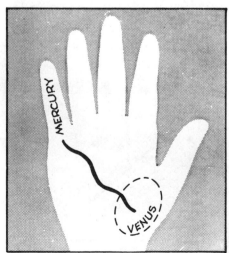

### -356-
### A wavy Line of Mercury starts inside the Mount of Venus and travels across the palm towards Mercury.

You want to get as much fun and enjoyment out of life as time permits. You have the tendency to form habits that are unhealthy. You also hold on to attitudes and thoughts that wear you out. You need to start floating past your bad feelings.

### -357-
### Your Line of Mercury begins on the Mount of Venus and slants to the Percussion.

Love is the Motor of your vitality. Your buoyancy, wit, and spirit dwindle when there is no love in the air. The most serious thing you lose when you feel no one loves you is your sense of purpose. Once you are secure in love, you recoup your direction in life.

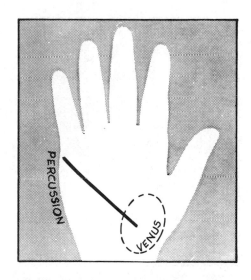

### -358-
### Your Mercury Line, which slants towards the Percussion, has a star formation on it.

You will have the good fortune of meeting a person whose love and consideration will help you evolve into a totally new person. The love this person gives you will direct you to become a person of action and discovery.

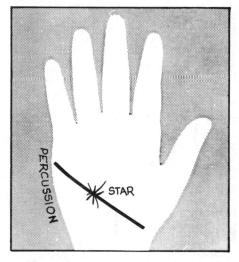

### -359-
### Your slanting Line of Mercury is intercepted by your Saturn Line.

Your spirit of aliveness and hopefulness is constantly held in check by your spirit of dread. Your overly cautious behavior will make you appear to others as stiff and formal. Old superstitions, which you have assumed from family members, limit your scope of activities.

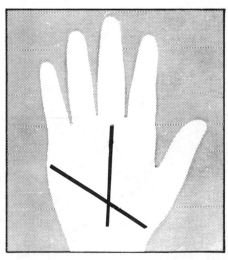

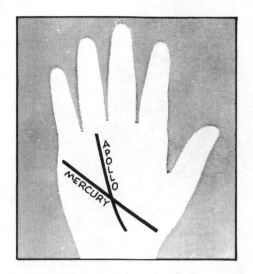

### -360-
### Your slanting Mercury Line intersects with your Apollo Line.

You are easily moved to tears on subjects of beauty and compassion. Your ability to succeed has its roots in your willingness to experiment. You are in the business of making the world beautiful.

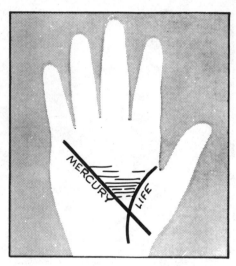

### -361-
### Many minor lines connect your Life Line and Mercury Line.

You may have already discovered that you have occult powers. This line formation indicates that you must remain very secretive about any of your extrasensory abilities. Your relatives and friends object to your use of occult powers. You have been hurt many times by others and are tempted to use your powers to get even.

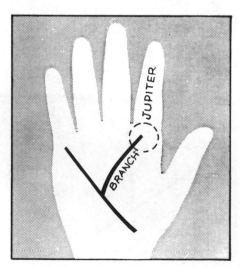

### -362-
### A branch leaves your Mount of Jupiter and joins your Mercury Line.

An upcoming business adventure thrusts you into the unknown terrain of the super rich. Until then, do not refuse the helping hands of friends. You show great leadership abilities and will eventually find satisfaction with this talent.

### -363-
### A branch from the Mount of Saturn falls to join your Mercury Line.

In many of the things you do, you view mostly the dark side and expect the worst. You rule out all those happy surprises. Your mind has a sober, conservative quality, and you hold very tight reins over all your actions. Your life is well planned from dawn till dusk. This particular palm line is a mark of success in the hands of people dealing with the exchange of cash.

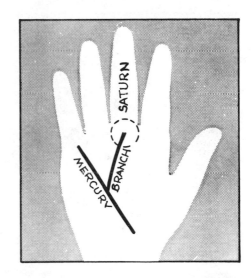

### -364-
### A branch from your Mount of Apollo joins your Line of Mercury.

You have an agreeable personality and are a shrewd thinker. People with this combination become independent in business.

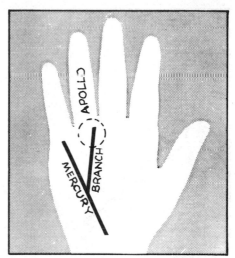

### -365-
### Your Line of Mercury terminates in a fork on the Mount of Mercury.

Your energies and time are split in half between two goals. A great success is awaiting you after choosing only one goal. One of your stronger talents might lie in a health-related occupation. Since you know how to make others happy, you might want to capitalize on this.

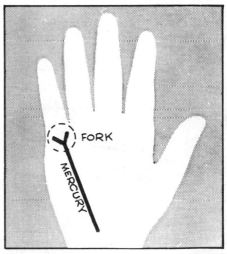

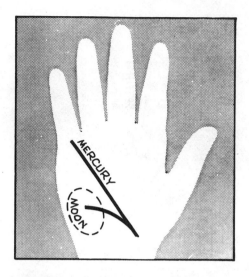

### -366-
### Your Line of Mercury sends a branch to the Mount of the Moon.

An involvement with a minor item of unimportance can lead to a disturbing obsession. You excel in handling the written word. You are a person who loves trivial details. You could turn your fastidiousness into profit and strengthen all insecurities by becoming a master of the written word.

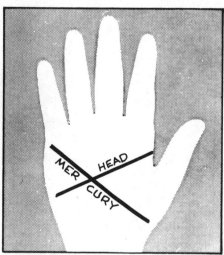

### -367-
### Your Line of Mercury forms a balanced "X" with your Head Line.

You fully possess the powers of the sixth sense. Learning to use these powers could put an end to your struggles. Some of your troubles are so inextricable that you were given these super powers to free yourself. No one is able to give you the answers you seek, and you will ultimately master these powers to free yourself of heavy burdens.

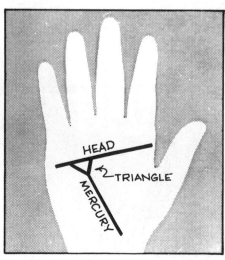

### -368-
### Your Mercury Line is forked at the end, and the fork meets your Head Line to form a triangle.

Deep-seated longings and cravings rule your logic. You try to satisfy them in all possible ways. Your temperament is colored by your single-minded drive to gratify these needs. The real source of these drives is a lack of intellectual fulfillment. Your mind needs the challenges which it often does not get.

### -369-
### A branch from your Line of Mercury shoots upward and merges into your Head Line.

A literary or scientific career is the calling for which you are cosmically suited. Your love of detail and puzzle-solving could also be woven into the fabric of a successful career. Besides mental brilliance, this configuration denotes power over others. Because you are a keen observer you can oftentimes diagnose and cure your own illnesses.

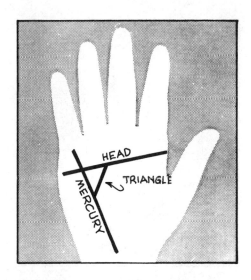

### -370-
### Your Line of Mercury begins close to the wrist, near the Life Line, but separates from it.

You know the secret of listening to your own body. You sense when the fine mechanisms of your body aren't attuned. Over the years you have picked up some good healthy habits, which will help you live to a ripe old age. Proper relaxation is an important factor. And to function properly you need more rest than most.

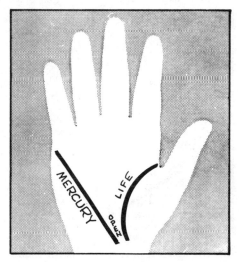

### -371-
### Your Line of Mercury and your Life Line do not join and do not cross.

It is advised to keep silent with those who are not your sworn allies. Strive to build up your personality to the point that you unwaveringly stand behind what you say. You are striving for a higher degree of self-confidence. It has not arrived, because you have not as yet experienced the major successes in your work. You are advised to follow through on goals and promises.

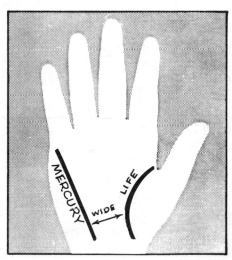

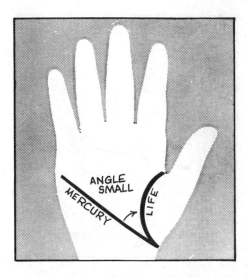

### -372-
**The angle formed between your Life Line and your Line of Mercury is small.**

You feel the need to collect things and to hoard. This makes up for the love that hasn't been granted you. You have a good heart and would do anything for a friend. You are often discouraged with friends, as you feel they do not give equally in return.

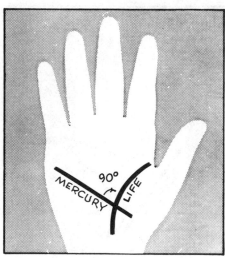

### -373-
**A right angle is formed by the intersection of your Life Line and Mercury Line.**

You set strict rules for yourself and try to conform to them. You are extremely proud of your fidelity to causes. You strive to be an angel. You express your goodness in your generosity. Integrity means everything to you.

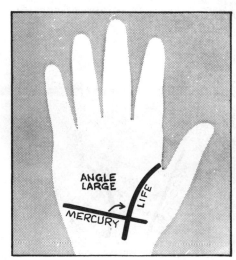

### -374-
**The angle formed by the junction of your Life Line and Mercury Line is obtuse (larger than 90 degrees).**

Some people with this line have a hard time getting up in the morning. Others would like to spend the rest of their lives snuggled in bed. Nighttime brings the hours of greatest creativity. You are impatient and lose your temper with persons you hold to be less intelligent than yourself.

### -375-
### The Great Triangle formed by your Head Line, Life Line, and Mercury Line has sides of equal length (a=b=c).

You have a well-balanced and moderately friendly disposition. Sufficient bravery backs your plans. You are reasonable and compromising in your dealings with others, while remaining firm and earning respect. You have mature reasoning abilities and hold resolutely to your principles.

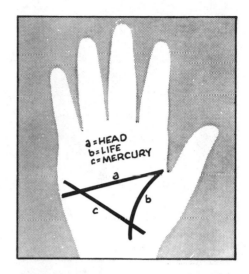

### -376-
### The Great Triangle formed by your Head, Life, and Mercury Lines is undersized.

You worry about unnecessary, petty details, which keeps you from finishing those important jobs on time. You are intolerant of yourself and are upset that you can't do all those things you want to. You are also afraid of decisions.

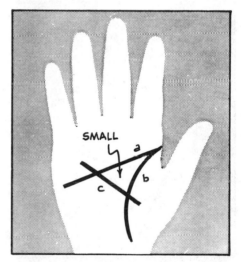

### -377-
### The Great Triangle formed by your Head, Life, and Mercury Lines is large.

The larger your triangle, the better your recuperative powers are. Your views of life are broad, and your field of action is ever expanding. You try to improve yourself, and every few years you evolve into an almost different person.

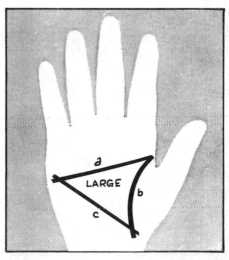

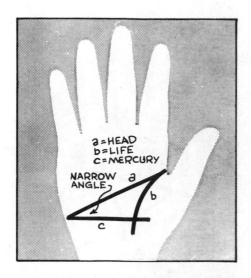

### -378-
**The upper left angle of your Great Triangle (formed by intersection of Head, Life, and Mercury Lines) forms an acute angle (less than 90 degrees).**

You are given to cautiousness. Your common sense and fair dealings with others makes you a dependable friend. Others rely on you too heavily for your own comfort. You dress carefully with a refined sense of taste for clothing and decor. Your stature is noble.

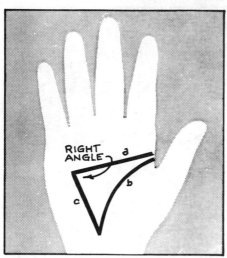

### -379-
**The upper left angle of your Great Triangle (formed by intersection of Head, Life, and Mercury Lines) forms a clearly defined right angle (= 90 degrees).**

Your mind is always active with constructive, concrete thoughts. You like to apply what you discover to practical projects. You have an accurate judgment for dimensions and proportions. You like to putter with your hands on complicated projects.

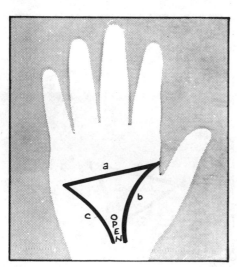

### -380-
**The bottom angle of your Great Triangle (formed by the junction of your Head, Life, and Mercury Lines) is barely joined.**

Activities and doingness form an integral part of your personality. You love being occupied. You are always on the go. You aren't satisfied until you are busy. Professional sports give you great satisfaction.

### -381-
### Your Saturn, Head, and Mercury Lines join to form a triangle.

This constellation denotes that you have a natural aptitude for the study of intricate details. You also understand innately the natural harmony governing our universe. You love nature and also have a green thumb.

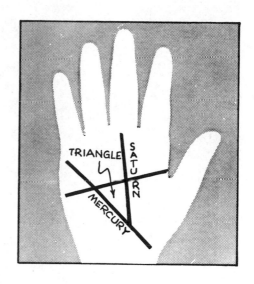

# THE MOUNTS

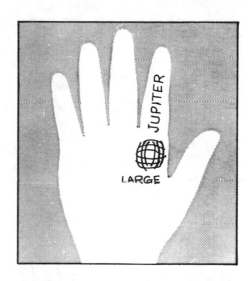

### -382-
### Your Mount of Jupiter (cushion of flesh under your first finger) is well developed.

You hold your feelings of love in proper perspective. Gaiety and humility are traits that make you well liked. You are also gifted with the power of good speech, which impresses others. Good living and comfortable surroundings are important to you. You have what some people call "old-world charm."

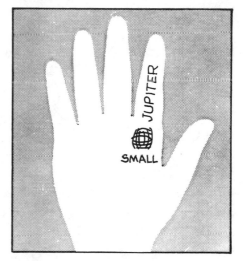

### -383-
### Your Mount of Jupiter (cushion of flesh under your first finger) is only slightly elevated.

You lack the pride and personal dignity which you have rightfully earned. You feel downhearted because you haven't accomplished all the things you set out to do. Your sensitivity is eroding your self-confidence. Impress upon your mind that "respect" is your birthright, and you will feel more confident.

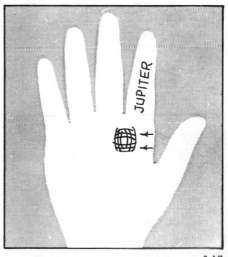

### -384-
### Your Mount of Jupiter (cushion of flesh under first finger) is displaced to the left.

Behind your assets of leadership—forceful communication of knowledge, love of authority and ability to teach—is a sensitive personality that has a different way of looking at things. You are out of step with your peers, because you search for wisdom and knowledge.

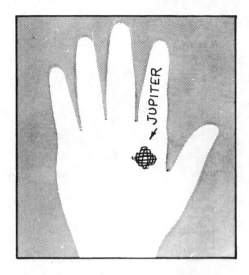

### -385-
### Your Mount of Jupiter (cushion of flesh under first finger) is displaced towards the center of palm.

You are more conscious than most people of yourself, your inner workings, and your feelings. This introspection causes you to be overly self-critical and easily alarmed. Getting absorbed in projects that are fun to do could help you to forget self. You gather much wiseness through your reflections, and the time will come when you share it with others.

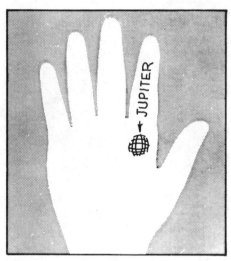

### -386-
### Your Mount of Jupiter (cushion of flesh under first finger) is displaced towards Lower Mars.

You have an irresistible temptation to dominate others. Someone spoiled you, letting you have your way for a long time. You have a high opinion of yourself and become inflamed when contradicted. You like to win over the opposition.

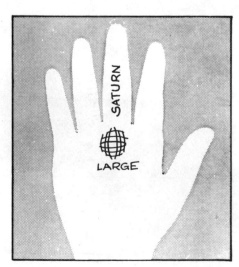

### -387-
### Your Mount of Saturn (flesh cushion under second finger) is well developed.
This elevation lends seriousness and caution to your character. You tend to believe that things do not change for the better, and wait apprehensively for eventual doom. You believe that spending your time in quiet, secluded places will rejuvenate you, but spending your time in good company will do a faster job.

### ✗ -388-
### Your Mount of Saturn (flesh cushion under second finger) is small.

You slip easily into melancholy and live in mild fear of something. You are not enjoying life as much as you could because of your foreboding attitudes. If you face the phantom, you will be a changed person. Placing too much importance on loyalty causes you to lose friends. You have firm, immovable religious convictions.

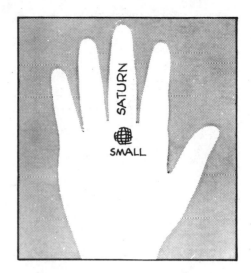

### -389-
### Your Mount of Saturn (flesh cushion under second finger) is displaced towards Jupiter.

Your good-natured disposition and your self-assuredness attract others, who are drawn to you in search of hope and consolation. By steadily building your self-confidence, you make steady progress in life.

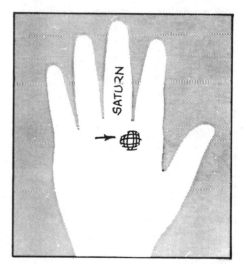

### -390-
### Your Mount of Saturn (fleshy cushion under second finger) is displaced towards Apollo.

This shift causes the more somber side of your personality to be softened. You develop a love of solitude and profit from a routine of peaceful contemplation. You have very strong, positive, recurrent thoughts that should be put into action.

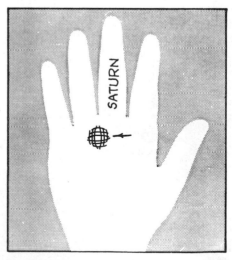

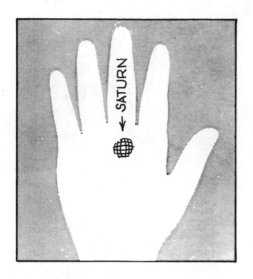

### -391-
### Your Mount of Saturn (fleshy cushion under the second finger) is displaced towards the Heart Line.

You hold on to your broken-heart memories. The longer you do so, the more callous and less compassionate you will become. If you return to the living you will wake up happy again. Your natural affections are crowded out by revenge and sorrow.

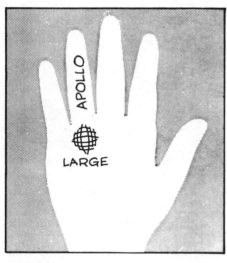

### -392-
### Your Mount of Apollo (fleshy cushion under third finger) is well developed.

You have the desire to shine before the eyes of others. You are enthusiastic about the beauty of all things. You want to build a beautiful home and surround yourself with objects of art. Your taste is generous and luxurious. Your nature is bright and sympathetic. You find and create beauty in the dimmest corners.

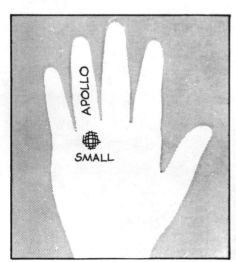

### ✗ -393-
### Your Mount of Apollo (fleshy elevation under third finger) is small.

Although you are materialistically inclined and want double security for your future, your bleeding heart impoverishes you. You tend to go on a shoestring to help needy friends. Although you are excellent in business, somehow you end up making those fortunes for others. By sticking up for the underdog you eventually become the underdog.

### -394-
**Your Mount of Apollo (fleshy cushion under third finger) is displaced towards Saturn.**

Boundless love for children and pets keeps the parental instinct in you alive. Your nature is gentle, warm, and patient. To keep your life balanced, you need a daily portion of love, and become perplexed when deprived of it.

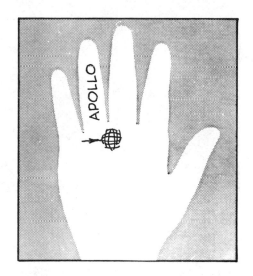

### -395-
**Your Mount of Apollo (fleshy cushion under third finger) is shifted towards Mercury.**

This displacement indicates a love of material possessions. You tend to care for animals more than for children. You shy away from facing situations that require your total commitment, and cherish your freedom above the pleasures derived from close family ties.

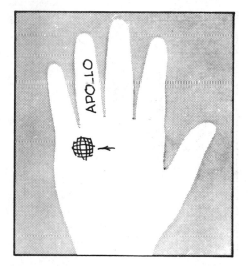

### -396-
**Your Mount of Mercury (fleshy padding under fourth finger) is well developed.**

You are intelligent, eloquent, and quick to react. You have unexplored reaches of the mind and could possibly excel in an intellectually stimulating field. You do not have a fixed notion of what you want to do in life and could change your plans or occupation at a moment's notice.

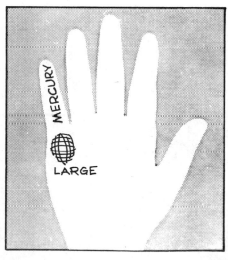

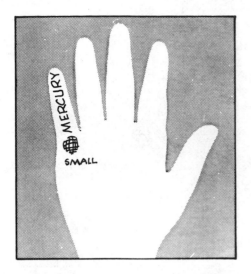

### -397-
**Your Mount of Mercury (fleshy cushion under fourth finger) is small.**

Your spirits are low and your self-esteem is sinking. You listen to your friends and relatives, and their notions drive you crazy. You want to rise above your self-deprecating attitudes but somehow end up with the wrong company. You need to learn to care less about what others think of you.

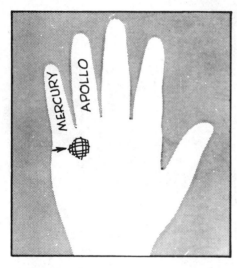

### -398-
**Your Mount of Mercury (fleshy bulge under fourth finger) is shifted towards the Apollo finger.**

This tends to create a character that takes life lightly. You consider the things most people worry about to be ridiculous. People ridicule you for not being more realistic, but you don't care. You know the score, and sometimes you only laugh things off as a mode of relief.

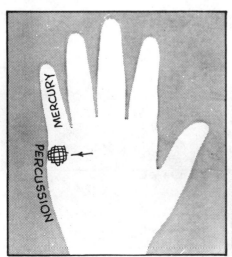

### -399-
**Your Mount of Mercury (fleshy bulge under fourth finger) is shifted towards the Percussion of the hand.**

This displacement lends to your personality a dash of courage. You have the capacity to work under strain without fear. You are quick to react, and are undaunted by the shocks life brings with it.

### -400-
**Your Mount of Mercury (fleshy cushion under fourth finger) is shifted towards the Heart Line.**

This marks your ability to rise in times of crisis to meet an emergency. You exhibit excellent spirit and audacity in situations where others would lose their heads in panic. You have dreams of combining your courage with a practical activity to relieve the chaos and suffering in the world.

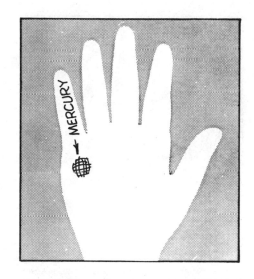

### -401-
**Your Upper Mount of Mars (Mount beneath the Mount of Mercury) is well developed.**

A large mound of flesh here lends courage, resistance, and an attraction to danger to your life. With a calm courage you can maintain an even temper during an upheaval. You do not yield easily. You are accustomed to having your own way. Sometimes you feel you are indestructible.

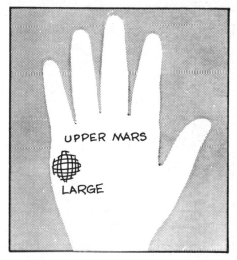

### ✗ -402-
**Your Upper Mount of Mars (Mount beneath the Mount of Mercury) is small.**

You have difficulty accepting responsibility. Hasty reactions without proper planning bring regrettable changes to your life that take years to clear up. You yield easily to the pressures from the outside. You feel you are only making dim progress in life.

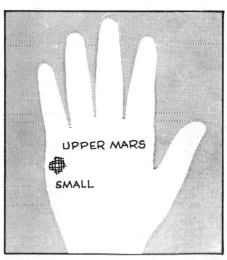

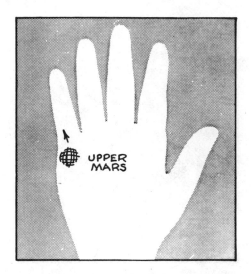

### -403-
### Your Upper Mount of Mars (Mount under the Mount of Mercury) is shifted towards the Mount of Mercury.

This is a fortifying sign. You have tremendous powers of endurance, saying "NO" to defeat at all times. You succeed in your life's goals, not because of any lucky openings, but because you stop at nothing to accomplish what you set your mind on.

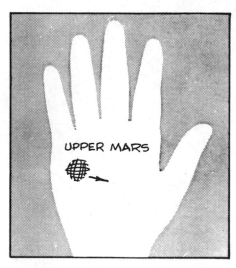

### -404-
### Your Upper Mount of Mars (Mount under the Mount of Mercury) is shifted towards the center of the palm.

This little bulge lends to your character an aggressive and courageous front. You are tempted to explore this side of yourself. Your character undergoes a complete change once you start doing those things that frighten you most.

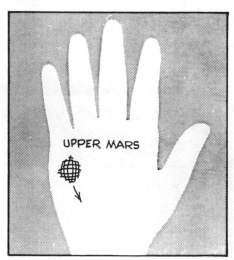

### -405-
### Your Upper Mount of Mars (Mount under the Mount of Mercury) is shifted towards the Moon.

People judge you as meek, but you aren't. Your tremendous patience and tranquility is often mistaken for shyness. It is really an enormous inner reserve. Your eyes and voice instill peace in those you encounter. You have hypnotic powers.

### -406-
### The uppermost portion of your Mount of Moon (fleshy padding on heel of hand) is developed.

Your mind is rich with images and colors, and is at the same time structured and orderly, so that you are adept at handling new and difficult situations. You would be well suited for a profession where you could put your originality and freshness to use. You blossom as a teacher or author.

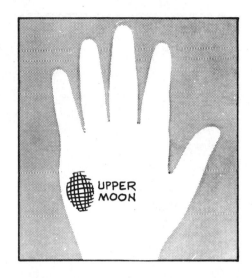

### -407-
### The middle portion of your Mount of Moon (fleshy cushion on heel of hand) is developed.

Your aptitude for business is strong. You are striving for a self-made business in which you can join your creativity and imagination with the logistics of business.

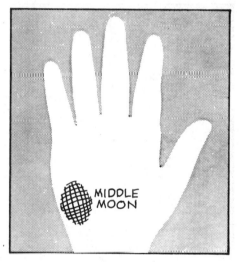

### -408-
### The lower portion of your Mount of Moon (fleshy cushion at heel of hand) is developed.

You have a continual yearning for the impossible and impractical. Your imaginative faculties are very well developed—so well, in fact, that often your imagination will take the upper hand and provoke you to live out fantasies in which you can escape from reality.

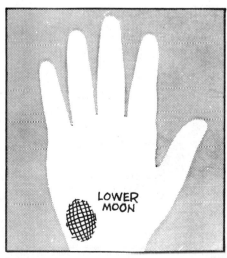

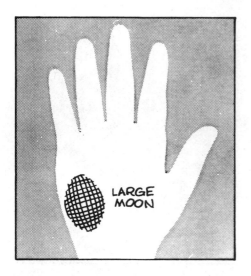

### ✗ -409-
### Your Mount of the Moon (fleshy padding at heel of hand) is large.

The size of this Mount is a reflection of the dimension of your imagination and sentimentality. You have a basic requirement in life for lavishly beautiful surroundings. You would travel a lifetime in search of the perfect setting of harmony in which to live. You are introspective and often prefer to listen rather than to speak.

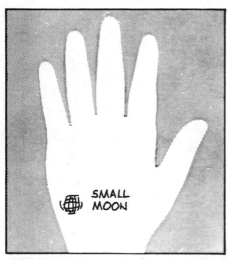

### -410-
### Your Mount of Moon (fleshy cushion on heel of hand) is small.

You are restless, searching for your niche in life. You feel empty and oftentimes live your days counting the hours. By surrounding yourself with inspiring people you get flashes of new ideas. You are waiting for that special moment that will make up for past failures.

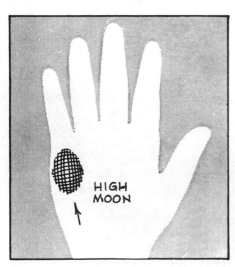

### -411-
### Your Mount of Moon (fleshy cushion at heel of hand) is shifted higher than average.

This reveals a very active and forceful imagination. Driven by an artistic, creative urge, you seek harmony as your main theme. This sign also marks your inventive abilities. You try to hold your imagination under strict rein, thereby producing sound, mature ideas that are saleable rather than wild, useless fantasies.

### -412-
### Your Mount of Moon (fleshy cushion at heel of hand) is shifted towards the outer edge of your palm (the Percussion).

With the gift of imagination this formation also brings the seed of envy, which brings you unrest. Your imagination plays tricks on you, exaggerating the ingredients of jealousy. You are on guard, protecting yourself against others, even the faithful.

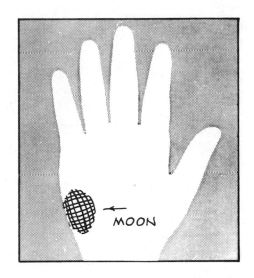

### -413-
### Your Mount of Moon (fleshy cushion at heel of hand) is displaced towards the wrist.

You have a wild and vivid imagination. You succumb easily to your daydreams and to suggestions. This "wanting to be somewhere else" side of your personality needs to be pushed into the background so that a new, fresh inspiration can be cut loose.

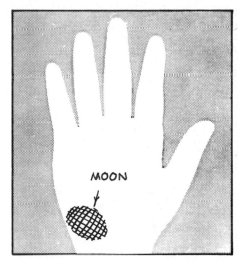

### -414-
### Your Mount of the Moon (fleshy bulge at heel of hand) is shifted towards the Mount of Venus.

Your imagination triggers emotional reactions, which in turn trigger worse imaginings. You oftentimes fall victim to your emotional fantasies. You need to stand up and face your dreads, and you will experience a joyful release without equivalence.

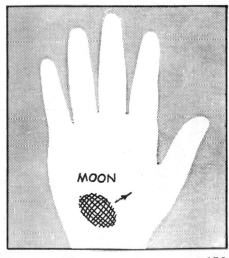

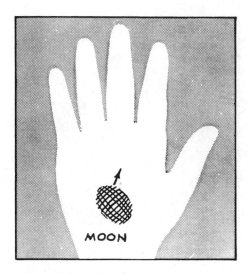

### -415-
**Your Mount of the Moon (fleshy bulge at heel of hand) is shifted towards the middle of the palm.**

You are in possession of a certain power to lead and control people. You are alert, react quickly, and have solid ideas. A combination of aggressive and imaginative forces advances you in your career at a rapid pace.

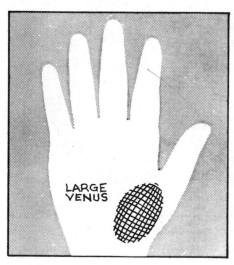

### -416-
**Your Mount of Venus (fleshy padding at root of thumb) is well developed.**

By nature you are very generous. The great moving forces in your life are affection, love of melody, gracefulness, and tenderness. This size mount is often associated with a talented singer or performer, whose expertise in rhythm creates joy in others. Your motivation expands the greater you are loved.

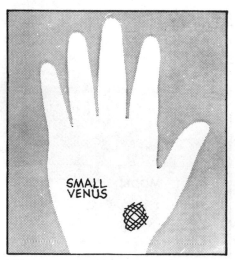

### -417-
**Your Mount of Venus (fleshy bulge under the thumb) is small.**

By lessening your social contact, you lose enjoyment in life. You have the need to surround yourself with beauty and splendor in order to replenish your feelings of loss.

### -418-
### Your Mount of Venus (fleshy bulge at root of thumb) is situated closer to your thumb than is the rule.

Your emotions dominate your will. Your disposition is often too emotional to leave room for logic. You want to get out from under the sway of your emotions, and you want to re-condition yourself to respond to logic and presence of mind. Once you direct yourself towards the selection of a clear goal, many interferences will drop away.

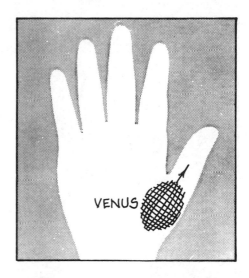

### -419-
### Your Mount of Venus (fleshy bulge at root of thumb) is situated closer to your center palm than is the rule.

This adds fire to the vital forces which drive you. You are sensuous, fond of luxury and comforts. You derive unending pleasure from the sensations of the physical world, and indulge in rare and choice foods. You are both wicked and tender.

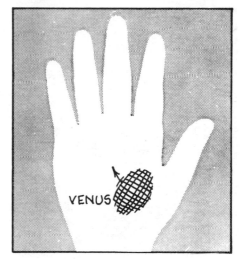

### -420-
### Your Lower Mount of Mars (fleshy padding near web of thumb) is well developed.

You take an active part in life and show a great deal of self-control and a great hidden reservoir of strength. You pursue your goals with an initial burst of energy. You accept impossible tasks just to prove to yourself you can do it. In testing your endurance, you sometimes push too far.

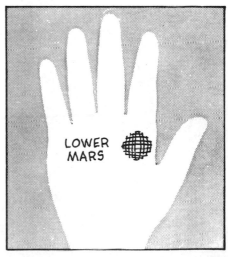

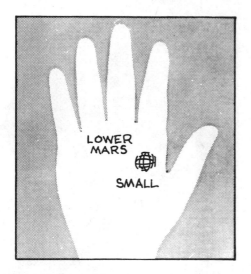

### -421-
**Your Lower Mount of Mars (fleshy padding near the web of thumb) is small.**

You shy away from any task that demands a display of courage. You have locked yourself up to protect yourself from the demands of life. You need to step outside of your protective shell and start firing up that old courage. The rule "the more you do, the more you can do" applies directly to you.

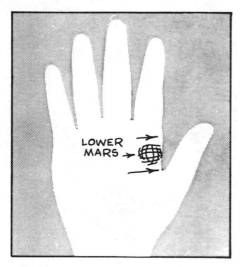

### -422-
**Your Lower Mount of Mars (fleshy bulge under Mount of Jupiter near web of thumb) is shifted towards the side of your hand.**

Your courage is the product of sheer willpower and grit. Once your mind is made up, nothing can change it, not even physical force. You fight back, sometimes using the limits of your energy.

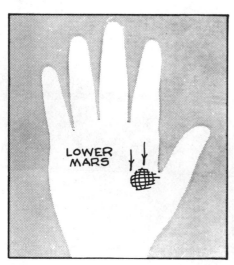

### -423-
**Your Lower Mount of Mars (fleshy bulge near the web of thumb) is shifted in a downward direction.**

Your power of endurance and bravery is directly related to the amount of attention and love you receive. When unhappy, you are powerless. Love gives you the staying power you need to meet life's crises.

### -424-
### Your Lower Mount of Mars (fleshy bulge near web of thumb) is shifted towards the middle of palm.

You have a tremendous attraction towards a daring lifestyle. You thrive on the tingle of danger. You are addicted to the thrills of a dangerous life and seek new ways to test your strength. You also show combative instincts.

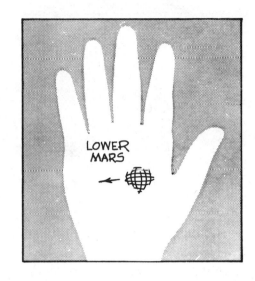

LOWER
MARS

# MARKINGS ON
# THE MOUNTS

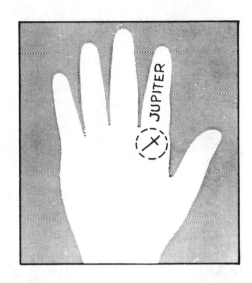

### -425-
### A cross is located on
### your Mount of Jupiter.

A new friendship filled with affection and sincerity takes you by surprise and alters your state of mind. You marry for love, not money. The higher you go in life, the more humility you show. You are restrained and polite.

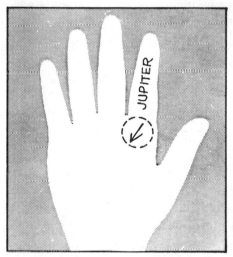

### -426-
### An arrow formation, pointing up or
### down, is on your Mount of Jupiter.

You wish to put the past behind you and be rid of memories and setbacks, and enter a happier time. You are looking for ways to revive yourself with new energies and put the exhilaration back into your life.

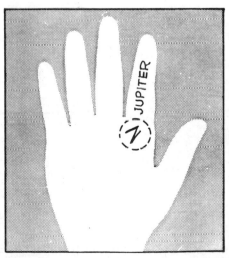

### -427-
### There is an "N" formation on your
### Mount of Jupiter.

You need an extra push to get started. For a long time you have relied on your good luck. If you would like to operate for more profit, you cannot rely on persons close to you for assistance or encouragement.

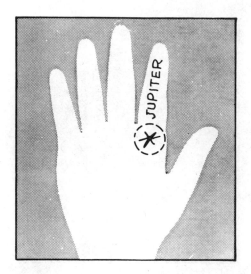

### -428-
### You have a star on the Mount of Jupiter.

You have the ability to speak and make yourself understood on a level that reaches everyone. An introduction to a distinguished person changes your life. You obtain that same distinction yourself and are spurred on to a heightened activity.

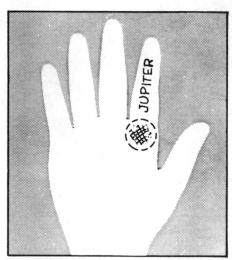

### -429-
### You have a grid on your Mount of Jupiter.

A force outside of you, stronger than you, is compelling you to gratify your ego. Frustrations mount, since you have chosen the impossible and are unable to face many things. You ask questions and seek answers to questions that are unanswerable. Your pride and your frustrations are barring you from matrimonial and other successes.

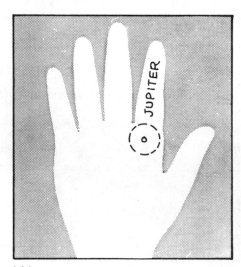

### -430-
### Your Mount of Jupiter has a circle on it.

Happy times are coming your way again. You receive a reward for distinguished efforts, which have gone unnoticed for a long time. This raises you to new heights and you become industrious. You feel stimulated to take up a new field of endeavor.

### -431-
### You have a triangle on your Mount of Jupiter.

You have an unusual talent for knowing what is right and just. The way you handle people makes them feel needed and appreciated. Your days are organized from early morning to late at night. You will never settle for less.

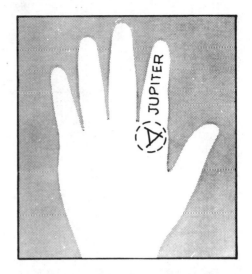

### -432-
### There is a square on your Mount of Jupiter.

You have surplus ambition which hasn't found the right channel yet. Any tiredness you feel could be due to this depletion of valuable energy reserves. The square will protect you from susceptibility to illness due to overexertion.

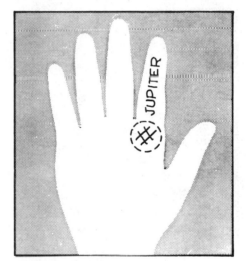

### -433-
### You have a cross on the Mount of Saturn.

You just don't overdo things, you go completely overboard and are exhausted long before your projects are ever completed. Often you give up just before the payoff. You are a planner. You plan trips or events months or even years in advance of their happening and execute them almost according to a timetable.

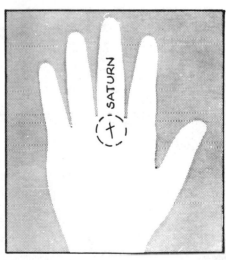

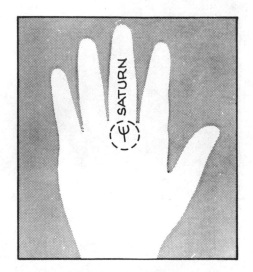

### -434-
### There is a marking resembling the Greek letter *psi* under Saturn.

You have the ability to change things using your psi powers. You need to use this power to lift yourself out of impossible situations. This psi power you have can also release you from feeling glum and dissolve nagging fears. Using the psi power, you can become rather wealthy later in life.

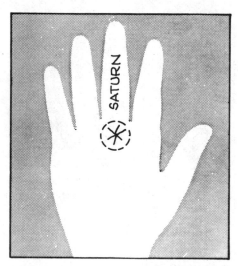

### -435-
### Your Mount of Saturn is starred.

A person of distinction and repute meets up with you. Together you try to make history. This person attempts to lead you astray, on the other side of the law. As you will be widely spoken of, it is better to stay on the right track.

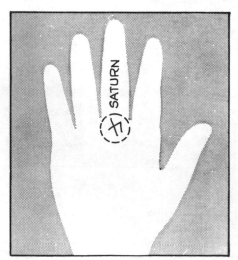

### -436-
### There is an upside-down "4" on your Saturn Mount.

You intuitively understand the mystical and philosophical lessons of life that others stumble through. Because of this knowledge you are spared life's greatest tragedies—those caused by stupidity. Therefore, you should devote concern towards the less fortunate.

### -437-
### Several short, parallel vertical lines appear under Saturn.

Each line symbolizes a crisis in your life that fragmented the order of things. As life proceeds, these fragments fall back into place, adding meaning to your life.

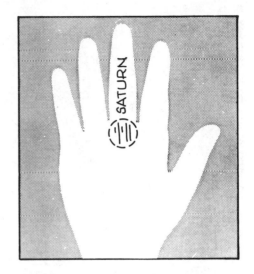

### -438-
### A grid formation is on your Mount of Saturn.

You are strongly melancholic and have to try twice as hard as others to achieve happiness. Often you find people irritating, as they do not understand your serious side. You have to work very hard in discovering your own personalized formula to achieve happiness.

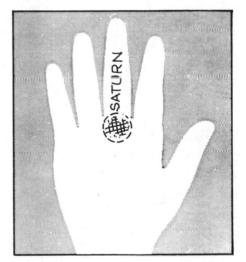

### -439-
### Your Ring of Venus ends on the Mount of Mercury.

Your overruling instinct is passion. No matter how hard you work against it, it still rules you. You are easily tortured by temptations and are a master at hiding these feelings from others. There is a side of you that no one knows.

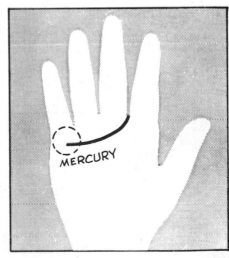

169

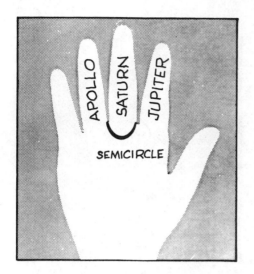

### -440-
**Your Ring of Venus forms a semicircle which rises between Jupiter and Saturn and ends between Apollo and Saturn.**

You are uncontrollably driven by a force in your life that causes you to do reckless things. You fall in and out of love easily. You make rigid demands of your lover, and when the signs of love wear off, you become embittered.

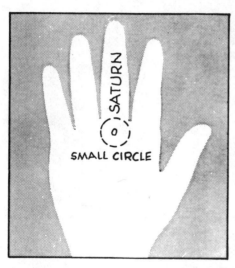

### -441-
**There is a circle on your Saturn Mount.**

You enrich your life through dealings with products of the earth, like minerals, earthenware, glass, gems, metals. You would do well in refining them, selling them, or using them in an artistic way. Involving yourself with the earth will also alleviate physical and emotional health problems.

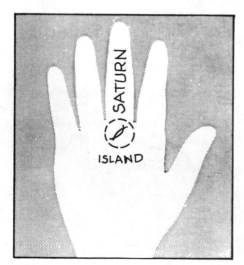

### -442-
**There is an island formation under Saturn.**

You are a naturally cautious person. Although you appear calm on the outside, you are always on the alert, because you do not like to be taken off guard. You feel the incessant need to protect yourself from unwelcome surprises.

### -443-
### You have a triangle on the Mount of Saturn.

You have a mysterious personality. People seldom fool you; you see right through them. You often have nobody to tell your troubles to. A gloomy, foreboding world has been opened up to you and has caused you inner agitation. You sense misfortune all around you and wish to use occult means to find relief.

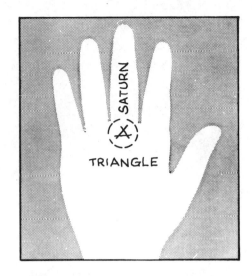

### -444-
### A square is located on your Mount of Saturn.

You have passed through many dangers with hardly a scratch. The square, in protecting you from future threats, cannot erase the shadows of the past nor protect you from them.

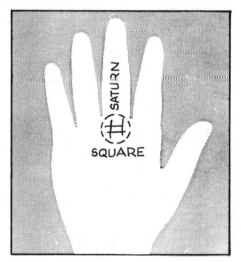

### -445-
### Your Marriage Line curves upward on the Mount of Apollo.

This is an enviable mark. You enter a union with an influential type. Your personalities work together to form a superb team. Both of you do more together than each of you would separately. You give rise to offspring who comes into the public eye through much favorable publicity.

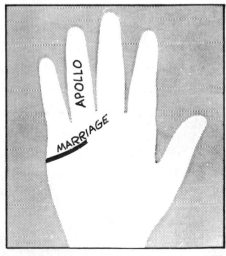

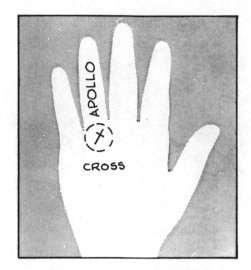

### -446-
### You have a cross on the Mount of Apollo.

You have tried very hard to reach real success and are now discouraged because of many blunders. You need to operate using a steady stream of energy—not too much and not too little—until you reach a humming balance. For optimal financial success you need to rid your life of deceit and envy.

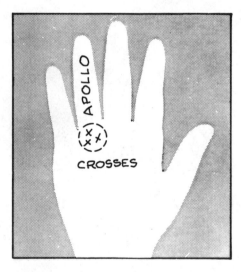

### -447-
### Little crosses are found under Apollo.

Marrying might bring you material advantages. Money gained through a marriage of this sort can be destructive unless combined with affection. Any envy or deceit you bring into this marriage will destroy your financial security.

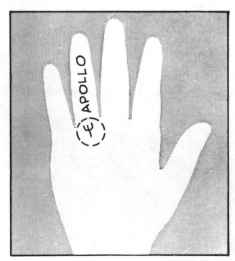

### -448-
### A sign resembling the Greek letter *psi* is under Apollo.

This is a favorable sign encouraging speculation in a daring new enterprise. This sign will help you make money without working too hard for it. This sign will also help you to find independence.

### -449-
### You have a star on the Mount of Apollo.

This is a sign that by freak chance a substantial pile of money will come your way. This also speaks of gaining illumination in a field that your natural instincts incline you to excel in (usually the arts). Because you have surplus strength in many areas you are likely to abuse your good qualities.

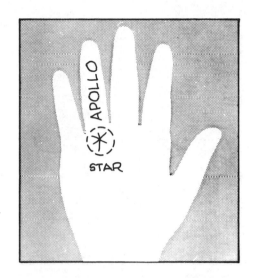

### -450-
### A grid formation is present under Apollo.

A grid in this position can sometimes be a menace. You try desparately hard to make your mark in this world and are very impatient, because your visionary idealism does not give you the results you expected. When you stop fighting your way to the top, you will be lifted there.

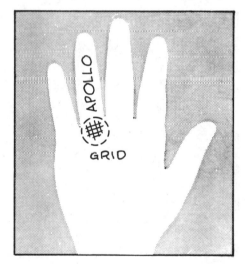

### -451-
### There is a circle under Apollo.

The circle is a very unusual sign. You are eager to finish what you start, and take up any smaller projects, leaving aside long-term projects. You like the feeling of success and like being in control, therefore you persist in short-range projects. This is also a sign that a fortune may be accumulated later in life.

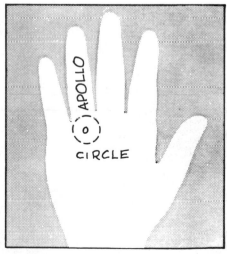

173

### -452-
### A Sun and Ray pattern is under your Apollo finger.

This sign is very rare. A worldwide reputation is in store for you. You are extraordinarily talented and strongly motivated. Your key to motivation comes by letting your curiosity lead you to discover the new and exciting. You are not easily confused.

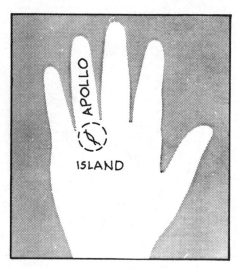

### -453-
### An island formation appears under Apollo.

Right now you are in an unfortunate position, and you are not willing to yield. You have had to change plans, and feel weakened in your confidence. You feel that beauty and love have gone out of your life, and this you miss terribly, because it is the wheel that turns you. You have the tendency to fall into lassitude, accepting your fate as permanent.

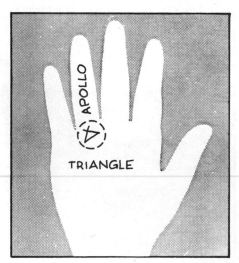

### -454-
### You have a triangle on your Mount of Apollo.

The triangle is a favorable sign, and located in this position it shows you have an aptitude for scientific pursuit. You also have an outwardly calm attitude and a natural attraction to people, and this makes you well suited to the medical profession.

### -455-
### There is a square on your Mount of Apollo.

Squares on the Mounts are a positive sign. They present a feeling of security. This square protects and preserves your enthusiasm and appreciation for the beautiful. The square will support you during setbacks. This sign also lends you the potential to make tremendous strides in a field of the arts.

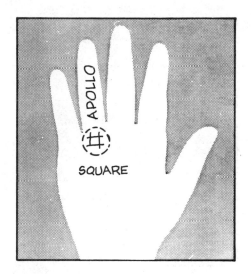

### -456-
### Your Line of Marriage is short and sturdy.

This line can refer to either a marriage or a liason. A short-lived, emotion-packed union is indicated, from which you draw much strength.

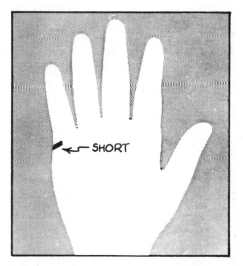

### -457-
### You have one clear, deep, straight Marriage Line.

This can only mean that you and another form a lasting relationship, festooned by mutual loyalty and trust. It will last as long as you wish it to, and a parting or separation of the two of you will be very difficult. Your affinity towards each other grows daily.

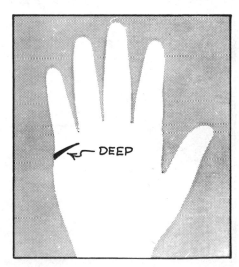

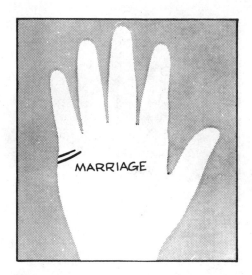

### -458-
### You have a Marriage Line with an overlapping line fragment.

This symbolizes a union in which there is a temporary rift. This rift can mean a growing period for you, a time for expansion, an enrichment. This bridges the marriage until it is permanently molded, and in the future there is a meeting of the minds on important issues.

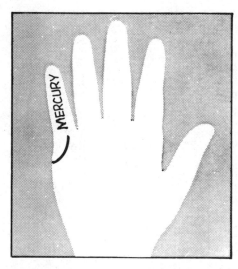

### -459-
### Your Line of Marriage curves upward on the Mount of Mercury.

You are not the "marrying kind." You are quite eager to be on intimate terms with the opposite sex. You are giving and generous and dutiful, but prefer an open-ended relationship that you can back out of at any time. You are a perennial romantic and thrive on the tingle of excitement of the newness of love.

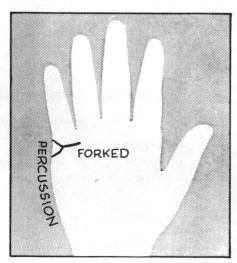

### -460-
### Your Marriage Line is forked at the Percussion.

A fork at the start means you were separated from your first true love, but eventually you reunite or find an equitable replacement. The separation caused you to grieve and feel irreparable loss. The joining of the fork to a single stem shows the eventual closeness and comfort that a true love brings.

### -461-
### You have a cross on your Mount of Mercury.

You feel star-crossed, as if fate had dealt you a bad hand. There are people you blame harshly for destroying your plans, and because of that, you give up projects easily. However, you still have spunk, wit, intelligence, and can push through to victory.

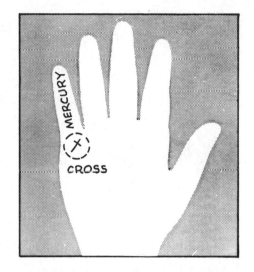

### -462-
### Your Marriage Line is cut by a descending line.

This signifies that people close to you are opposed to your romantic inclinations. You let yourself be influenced by what others deem is right for you. You long for excitement with your mate.

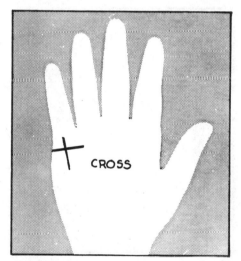

### -463-
### You have a star on the Mount of Mercury.

The Star of Brilliant Intellect is found in this position. It shows you have reasoning powers that are way above average. If you devoted your entire life to searching for an eternal truth or light, you would become a visionary. Some of your dreams become reality.

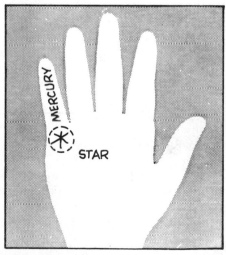

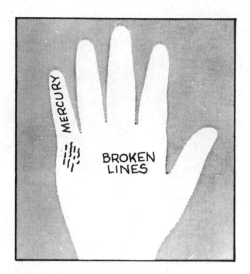

### -464-
### Many fragmented lines appear under Mercury.

You live a stormy life, torn between reality and your many hopes and dreams. You dilute your energy by attempting to do many things at once. You put aside activities that bring you enjoyment. Major changes are occurring within you that will bring you relief.

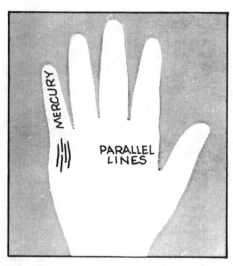

### -465-
### Parallel vertical lines descend from your Mercury Finger.

Your talents mostly lie in the area of caring for the less fortunate. You have deep compassion and understanding of the needs of the lesser endowed. Gaining new knowledge brings you great excitement. You do your greatest traveling in areas mostly of the mind.

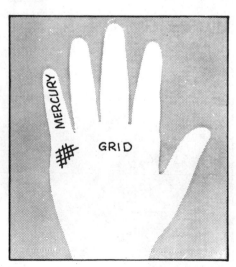

### -466-
### A grid appears on your Mount of Mercury.

It has taken you longer than most people to mature. Sometimes you feel you will always be a child inside. You don't feel confident carrying a heavy load of responsibility. You feel comfortable telling fibs to help you get out of situations that make you feel uncomfortable.

### -467-
### You have a triangle on the Mount of Mercury.

This is called the Triangle of Wittiness, and it is a symbol of daring talk and ready wit. You are adept at ad-libbing. This sign also means an aptitude for scientific pursuits. You are fascinated by logic and pure thinking. Your reactions are very quick, and you are not only mentally nimble but also physically quick to react.

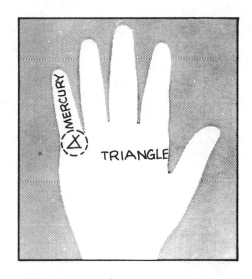

### -468-
### There is a square on your Mount of Mercury.

This is always a favorable sign protecting you from any possible harm. You need to be protected from losing your greatest asset: your clear, swift, bright mind. This square will also help protect your savings and will preserve your sanity in worrisome times.

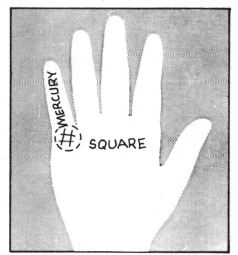

### -469-
### A horizontal line stemming from the Percussion runs across the center of the Mount of the Moon.

You will develop an urge to travel to the places that help you unravel your family history. You would like to understand your unconscious drives that make you act and think the way you do.

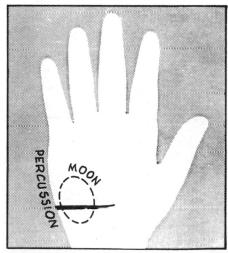

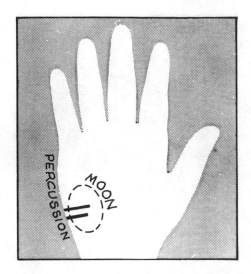

### -470-
### Several horizontal lines project onto the Mount of Moon from the Percussion.

These marks intensify your urge to travel. In your traveling you have an instinct to discover something that is obscure and remote. You have fine instincts for tracking down things hidden, and could be very effective if you combined this passion with a profession.

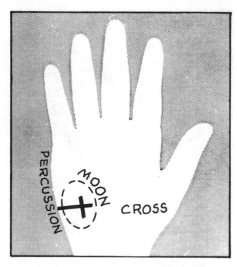

### -471-
### A horizontal line with a cross-bar stems from your Percussion and stretches across your Mount of Moon.

You are dismayed because you have been detained from going on the greatest adventure of your life. You would like to understand your unconscious better and unravel your vivid dreams, but someone is barring you from getting deeper in touch with yourself.

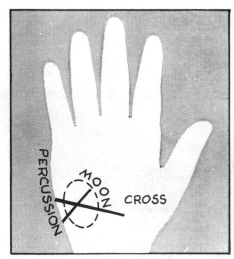

### -472-
### Two lines emerging from the Percussion run across your Mount of Moon and cross each other.

Your past seems like a far-off dream, and you have sought to understand it and your present preferences. You have tried diligently to get in touch with your past, and this has brought variety and change into your life. You are restless and not content with the mundane realities of this world.

### -473-
**A horizontal line from the Percussion crosses the Mount of Moon and has an island on it.**

You have an internal restlessness, and have a haunting feeling that you should be occupying your time differently. You yearn to get away, but somehow are thwarted in your attempts to gain freedom by a force that weakens you. You are cautioned to pay special care to your intestines and bladder.

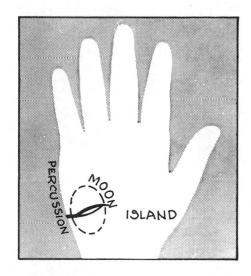

### -474-
**A horizontal forked line stretches from the Percussion across the Mount of the Moon.**

You might experience some problems of health, which are greatly exaggerated by your imaginings. You have a great yearning to travel and are fascinated by adventure. There is a great deal of indecision and change in plans surrounding travel plans.

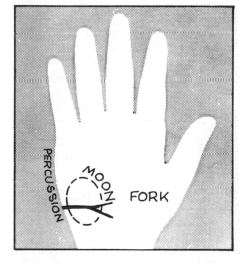

### -475-
**A horizontal line emerging from the Percussion ends in a triangle on the Mount of Moon.**

When being led by others you are reasonable and compliant. Your intuition and occult abilities lead you to travel thirsting for knowledge.

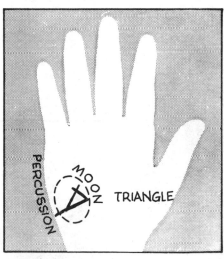

181

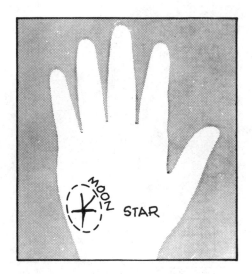

STAR

### -476-
### Your Mount of Moon has a star on it.

In the past this marking was an indication of a chronic sickness. There is also a school of thought that names this the Star of Brilliant Intellect, since this star in this position is also found on the hands of great thinkers and philosophers. People with this sign believe that the most important thing in this lifetime is the search for truth and light. Their visions often become the realities of tomorrow.

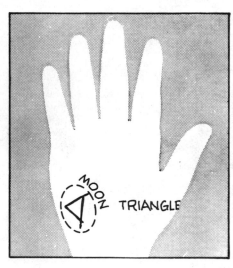

TRIANGLE

### -477-
### You have a triangle on the Mount of Moon.

A triangle in this position means that you have inherited a certain wisdom about sizing up people and knowing the outcome of things before they happen. This sign also means an aptitude for scientific pursuits. You have a very active imagination and aren't afraid to speak boldly.

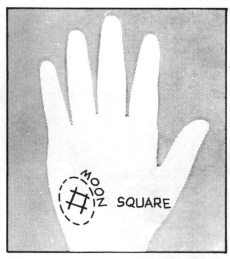

SQUARE

### -478-
### You have a square on the Mount of Moon.

This sign gives you the wisdom and intelligence and quick reflexes to ward off trouble before it becomes acute. This is a lucky sign to have if you are a businessperson who travels often. This sign will also protect you from injury when engaged in sports.

### -479-
### A cross on your Mount of Venus.

Constant battling with ones close to you wears you to a frazzle. You fear losing your right to be right, and hope that by winning arguments you will also win your self-esteem. Unfortunately this formula doesn't always work for you. This sign can also be called the "St. Andrew's Cross," which connotes that you will find a happy love affair with only one person.

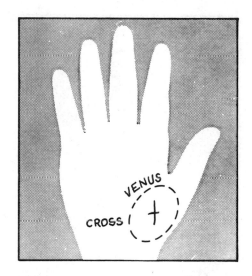

### -480-
### A star is located on your Mount of Venus.

You have an animal magnetism that keeps admirers swarming. Your sensuality is topped with affection and surging passion. You know how to keep several admirers on a string. Whenever there is love in your life, there is also trouble.

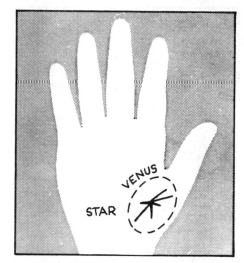

### -481-
### There is a star formation on your Life Line.

When you lost that person you loved most, you lost most of yourself. The feeling of being alone and lost takes awhile to heal. You emerge from a cocoon after a long period of withdrawal and experience life afresh.

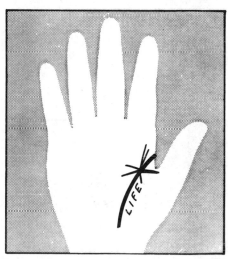

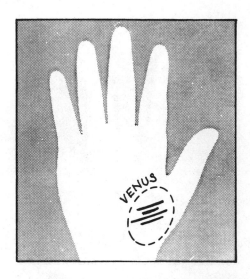

### -482-
### There are strong, deep lines on your Mount of Venus.

You do not always know how to express your gratefulness. Although others may regard you as unappreciative, you are really distracted or preoccupied. You are inwardly shy and find it difficult to relax. This is your main drawback to success.

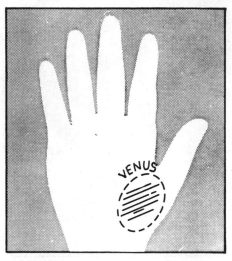

### -483-
### Many fine lines cross your Mount of Venus.

You are the sensuous type. Your refined, sensitive nature stands out as your most striking feature. The gentleness of your person may not always be visible on the outside, but it is always there, on the inside. You love colors, fragrances, fantasies, and the velvet life.

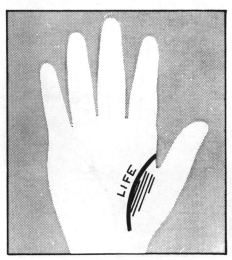

### -484-
### Many fine lines run parallel to your Life Line.

Ethical reason, traditions, and various excuses interfere with the success of your love life. You can be easily swayed by the opinions of others. You have not yet formed a permanent foundation for your personality, and need to build self-confidence in your favorite fields of interest through more exposure.

### -485-
### There is a grid at the base of your thumb.

You have always feared being separated from the one you love. You have an intensified need to be loved. There is often confusion in your love life. Much useless time is spent clearing away obstacles in the path of your love.

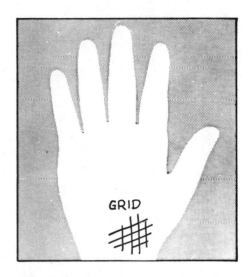

### -486-
### You have a grid in the center of the Mount of Venus.

Your moods are sometimes like a pendulum, and they swing out of control. You have witnessed many distressing unheavals, and now you are searching to stabilize your feelings. Towards the middle of your life you become more sexually active. Your trust in the order and logic of the universe needs to be rekindled. This can be achieved with the help of an understanding mate.

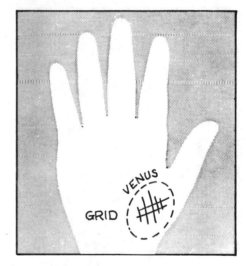

### -487-
### You have a triangle on the Mount of Venus.

You are a wise and cautious person. You are extremely choosy about whom you select as your mate. You know how to keep your partner's interest in love alive. A marriage must bring some reward to you, either material or mental.

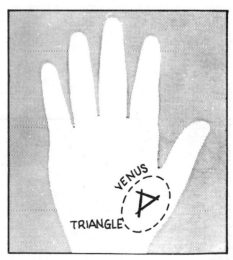

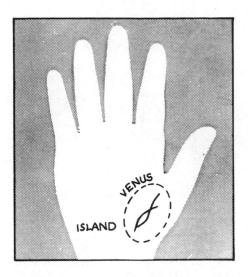

### -488-
### An island formation is on your Mount of Venus.

Not realizing it at the time, you passed up a very advantageous marriage or liason. If your onetime wooer is still in the vicinity, hasten to consummate the nuptials. People carrying this sign need to be reminded that only they can create a new tomorrow by efforts made today, no matter how minute they may be.

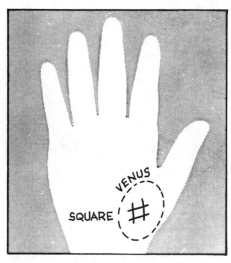

### -489-
### A square is on your Mount of Venus.

You experience a narrow escape from the law and are spared a life of disgrace. You have led a confining life up until now and crave expansion. To get yourself out of present constructions, you need to trust your instincts and remember that this sign of the square automatically will give you the security you need after you have made your decision.

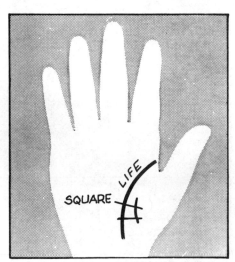

### -490-
### A square touches your Life Line.

You have the tendency to encapsulate yourself from the outside world. You regard your surroundings as a prison. It is time for you to work your way out and teach the world what you have learned. You would make a good public lecturer for a humanitarian cause by using your life's experience.

### -491-
### The letter "L" crosses the Life Line in the Lower Mount of Mars.

A prolonged disagreement between you and a family member has been an agonizing experience. You will come to the verge of ending the clash with brute force. Someone could be injured, and it is up to you to find an amicable settlement.

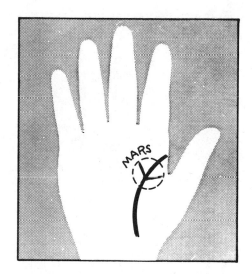

### -492-
### A star formation appears above your Lower Mars region.

Although the star is mostly a worthy sign to have, sometimes it is a bad sign, as in this case. An ongoing feud between you and an enemy might lead to a court settlement, which is not in your favor. To avoid losing, try to patch up old misunderstandings in a hurry. Only a little "give" is required on your part, and the opposition readily complies.

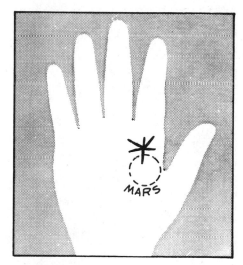

### -493-
### You have a star on your Lower Mount of Mars.

You could rise high in social status through your affiliation with the armed forces or a large public organization. By pursuing activities involving group interaction, your marriage is positively affected. You are attracted to activities that are hazardous.

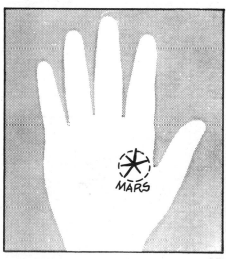

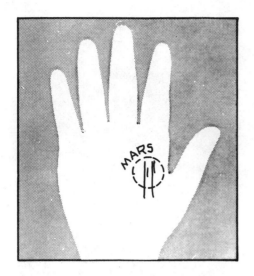

### -494-
### Thin lines originate from your Lower Mount of Mars.

You are easily swayed by the opinions held by the opposite sex. The effects are profound and influence the way you manage money and dress. You are not in complete control of your temper and have the capacity to swing into brutish actions.

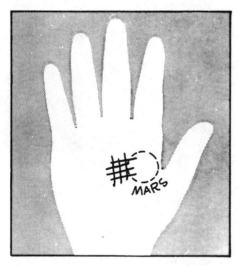

### -495-
### You have a grid near the Lower Mount of Mars.

Once you have gotten angry about something, it is very hard for you to shake this feeling. Your anger can mount until it is a seething, almost murderous, instinct that consumes you. If your later years are filled with a mission of significance, these feelings will recede, and in their place will come material and spiritual riches.

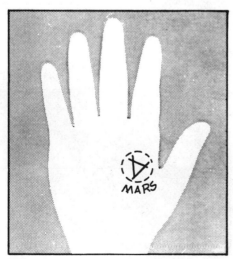

### -496-
### You have a triangle on the Lower Mount of Mars.

You have a strategical mind and are excellent at predicting a person's next move through his or her past actions. You also have a distinguished attitude of showmanship. Top military people and other leaders carry this sign.

### -497-
### You have a star on the Upper Mount of Mars.

You are a born fighter. Now your battles might be silent and without popular appeal, but one day you will be widely known for your courageous stand on worthwhile issues. Your success now largely depends upon your patience, which is not your greatest virtue. It is recommended that you stay away from sharp edges and firearms. You slip easily into moods of jealousy and wrath.

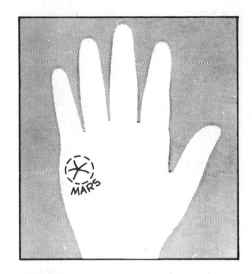

### -498-
### A star is present between your Head and Heart Lines, under your Mount of Mercury.

You possess descriptive, inquiring faculties and a love for accurate detail and precise reproduction. You could rise to great heights and achieve inner satisfaction if you put these talents to commercial use, as in the fields of banking, graphics, or science.

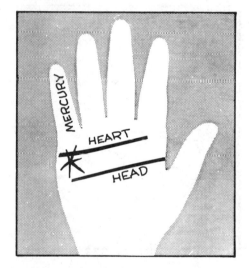

### -499-
### A triangle is on your Upper Mount of Mars.

This is an excellent sign to have. It lends you calmness in the face of real danger. You always have presence of mind in a crisis. This makes you dependable. You have an aptitude for strategy and tactics, like those of military leaders, and you would do well pursuing a career along these lines.

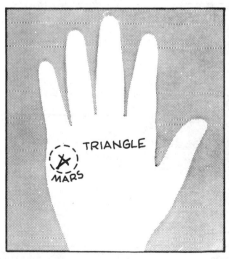

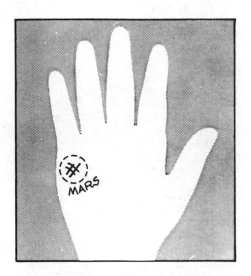

### -500-
### You have a square on your Upper Mount of Mars.

Any tendency you have towards violence and unpredictable outbursts will be held in check through this configuration. You are the type who must practice controlling your emotions through mind power. This square will also protect you from bodily harm during arguments.

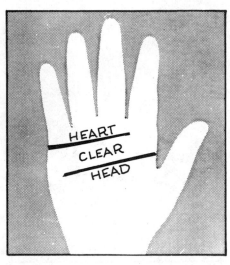

### -501-
### The space between your Head and Heart Lines is devoid of any markings.

This is important, as it tells of a calmness and presence of mind you have which is necessary in emergencies. You examine situations carefully but quickly before jumping into action. Your good judgment is sought often by friends and dependents.

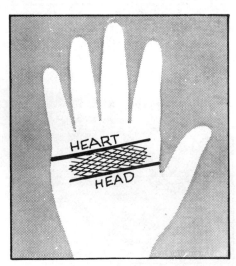

### -502-
### Hair lines appear in the space between your Heart and Head Lines.

Unnecessary frightfulness disturbs your balance. You are haunted by many fears, and most of them are needless. You are often restless and irritable for no apparent cause. You must rediscipline your mind to believe that you can change these habits.

### -503-
**There is a cross on your palm under the Mount of Saturn, between your Heart and Head Lines.**

This is known as the Mystic Cross. It signifies an intense longing for knowledge. The knowledge you are seeking is on many levels. Philosophers, attorneys, and church leaders often have this mark. You will have a trail of followers needing your support.

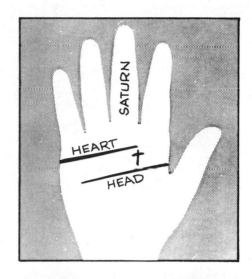

### -504-
**There are crosses between your Heart and Head Lines.**

This denotes a natural gift of mysticism. You take life seriously. You often look for signs of mystical significance. You are on the superstitious side. You have significant ability to write beautiful, mystical poetry.

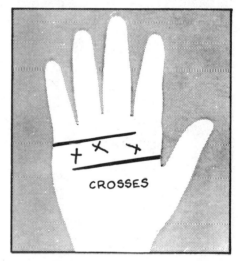

### -505-
**A star is present between your Head and Heart Lines, under the Mount of Apollo.**

Success is waiting for you in some aspect of the art of communication. You know how to win the appeal of those around you. You also understand the proper balance of courtesy and pressure to get the things you need from others. You handle large sums of money well.

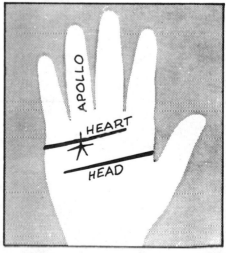

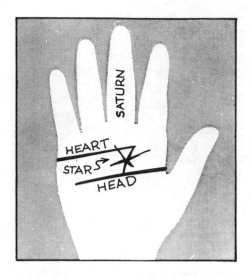

### -506-
### A star can be found between your Head and Heart Lines, under the Mount of Saturn.

You have an outstanding career ahead of you. You will master the art of concentrating your efforts to achieve one important goal. You are destined to teach others to help themselves. You understand the importance of change and accept changes gracefully.

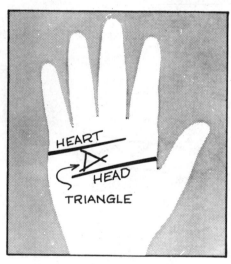

### -507-
### You have a triangle between your Head and Heart Lines.

You have an insatiable curiosity. Many of the types of questions you need answers for are unanswerable. You also want split-second answers. You prefer to have others confirm what you already know to be true before you proceed.

# Reference Guide

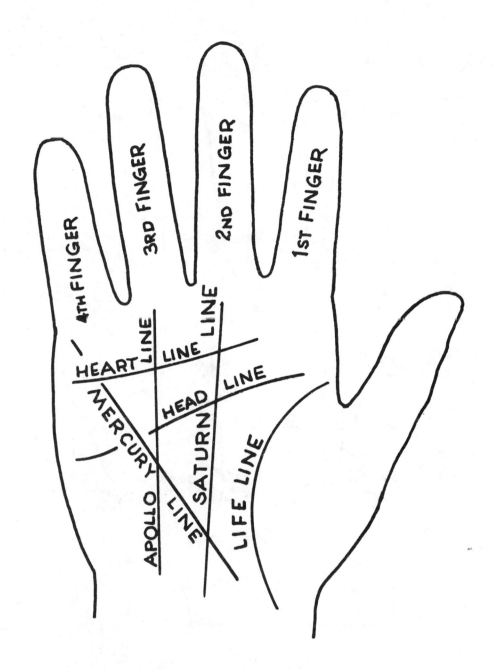

**MAIN LINES**

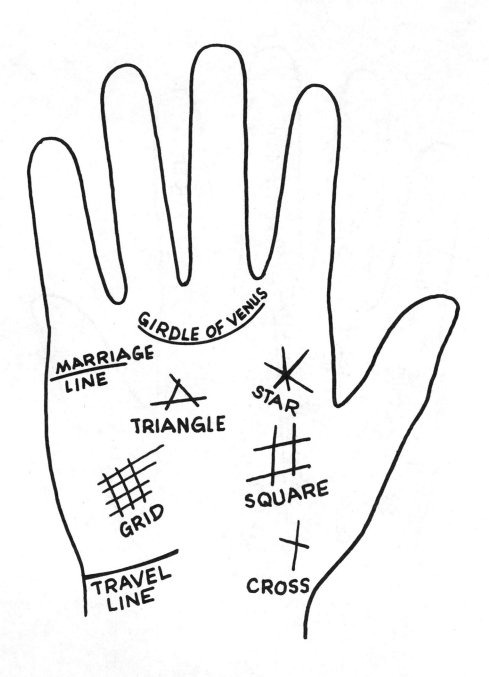

**MARKS**

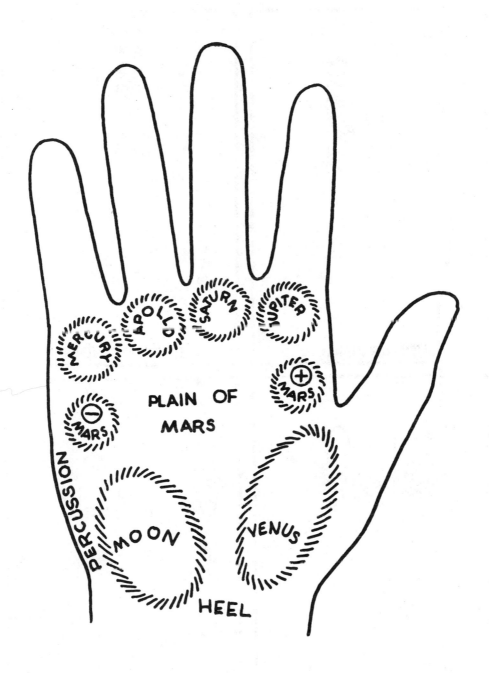

**MOUNTS**

# NAMES OF FINGERS

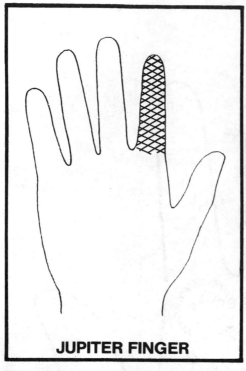

**JUPITER FINGER**

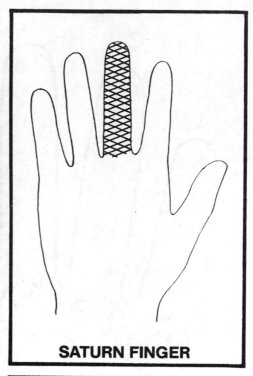

**SATURN FINGER**

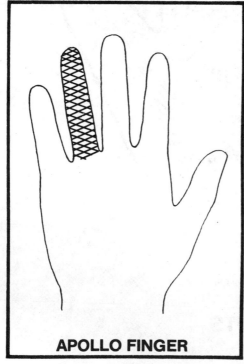

**APOLLO FINGER**

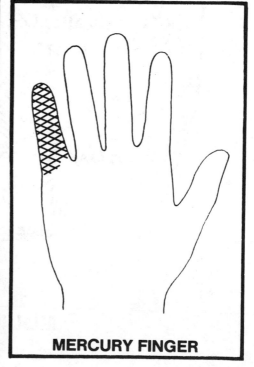

**MERCURY FINGER**

# NAMES OF FINGERS

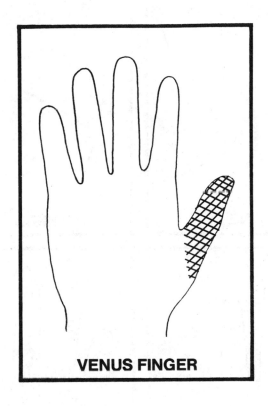

**VENUS FINGER**

# MAJOR LINES

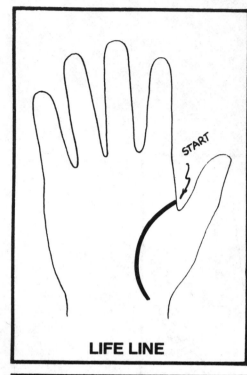

**LIFE LINE**

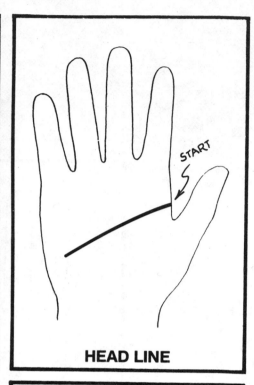

**HEAD LINE**

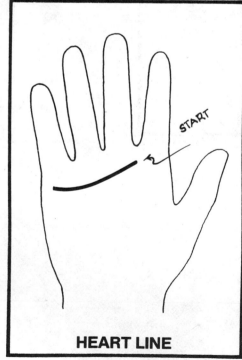

**HEART LINE**

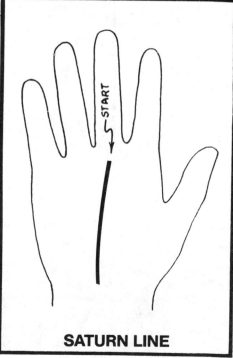

**SATURN LINE**

# MAJOR LINES

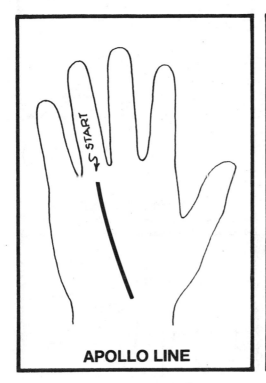

**APOLLO LINE**

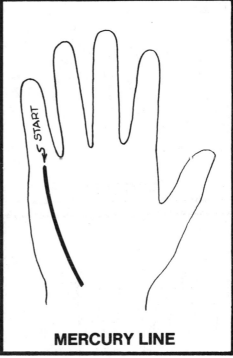

**MERCURY LINE**

# VARIATIONS IN LINES

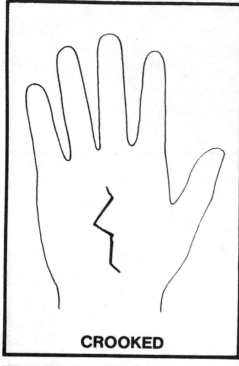

**CROOKED**

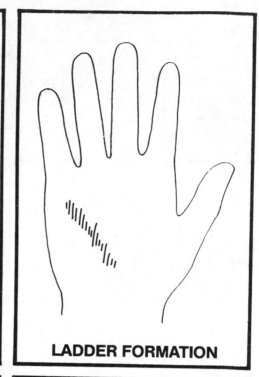

**LADDER FORMATION**

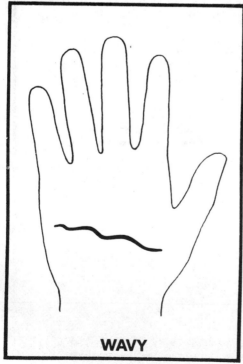

**WAVY**

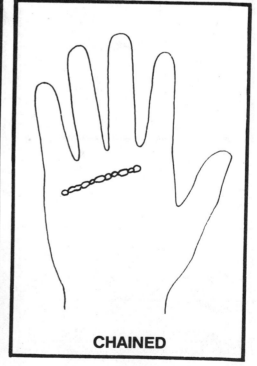

**CHAINED**

# VARIATIONS IN LINES

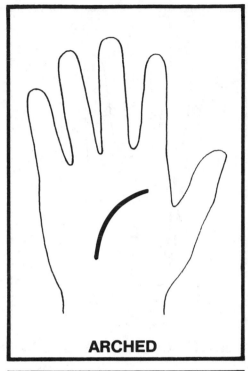

**ARCHED**

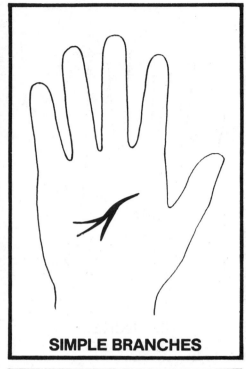

**SIMPLE BRANCHES**

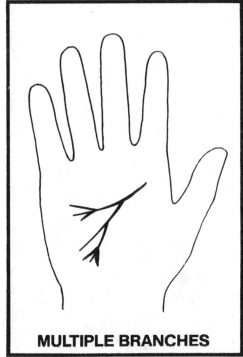

**MULTIPLE BRANCHES**

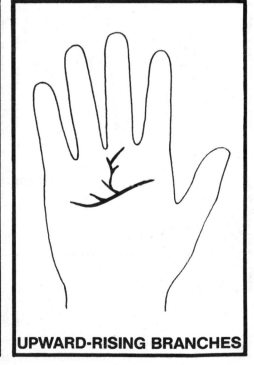

**UPWARD-RISING BRANCHES**

# VARIATIONS IN LINES

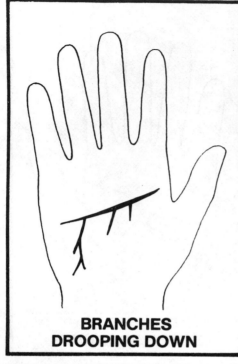

**BRANCHES
DROOPING DOWN**

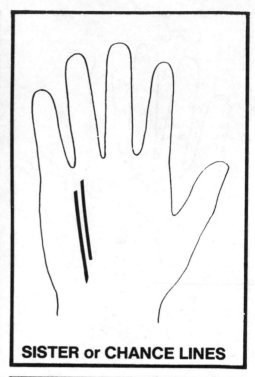

**SISTER or CHANCE LINES**

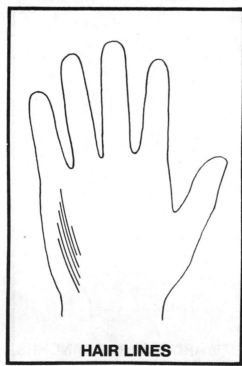

**HAIR LINES**

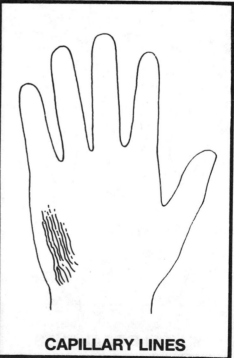

**CAPILLARY LINES**

# VARIATIONS IN LINES

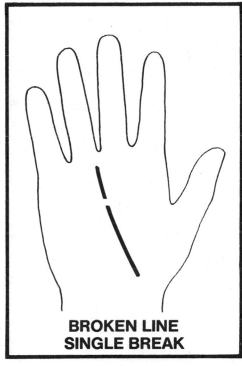

**BROKEN LINE
SINGLE BREAK**

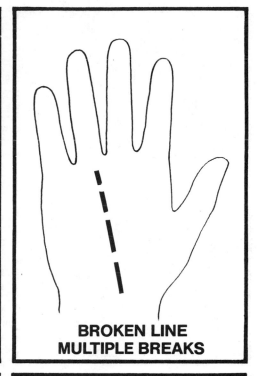

**BROKEN LINE
MULTIPLE BREAKS**

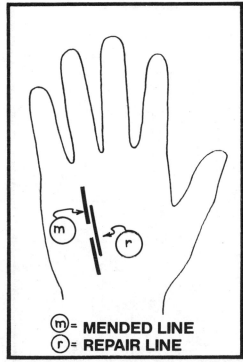

ⓜ= MENDED LINE
ⓡ= REPAIR LINE

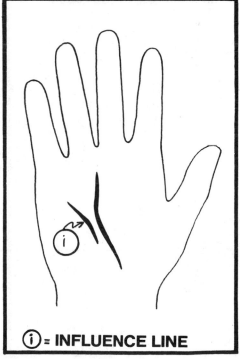

ⓘ= INFLUENCE LINE

# VARIATIONS IN LINES

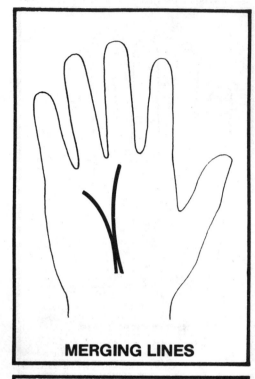

**MERGING LINES**

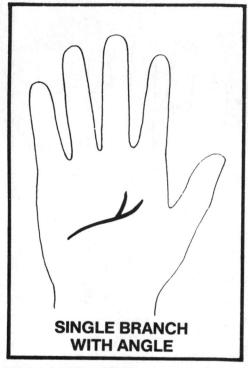

**SINGLE BRANCH
WITH ANGLE**

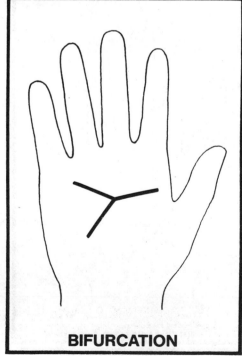

**BIFURCATION**

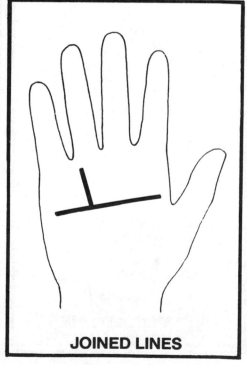

**JOINED LINES**

# VARIATIONS IN LINES

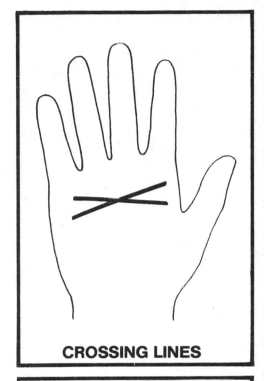

**CROSSING LINES**

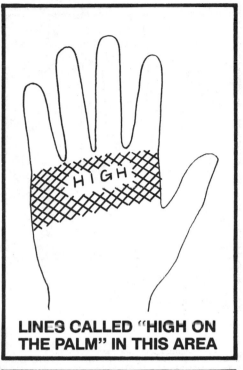

**LINES CALLED "HIGH ON THE PALM" IN THIS AREA**

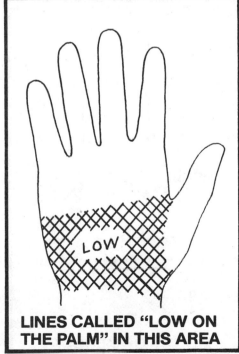

**LINES CALLED "LOW ON THE PALM" IN THIS AREA**

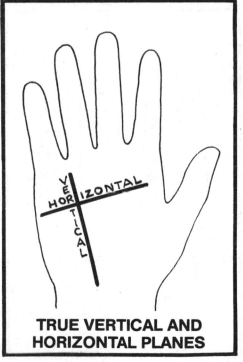

**TRUE VERTICAL AND HORIZONTAL PLANES**

# NAMES OF MOUNTS

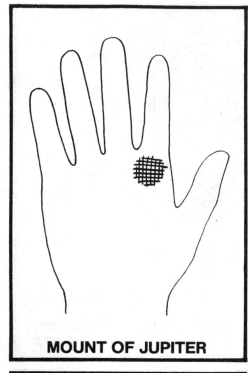

**MOUNT OF JUPITER**

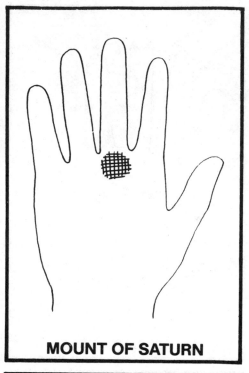

**MOUNT OF SATURN**

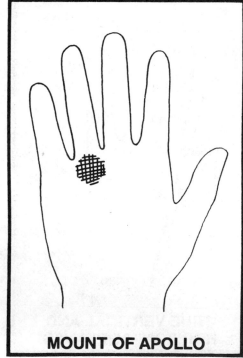

**MOUNT OF APOLLO**

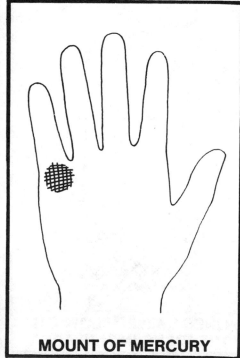

**MOUNT OF MERCURY**

# NAMES OF MOUNTS

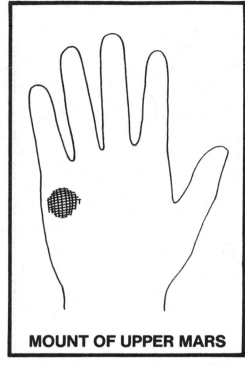

**MOUNT OF UPPER MARS**

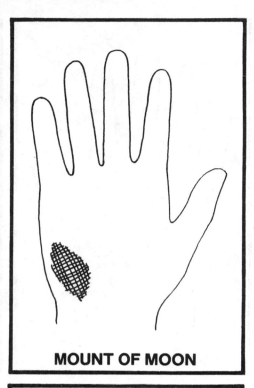

**MOUNT OF MOON**

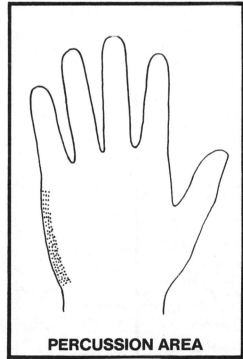

**PERCUSSION AREA**

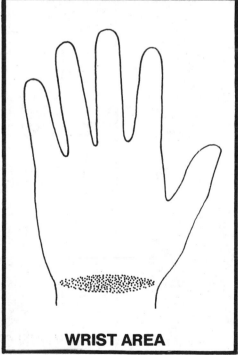

**WRIST AREA**

# NAMES OF MOUNTS

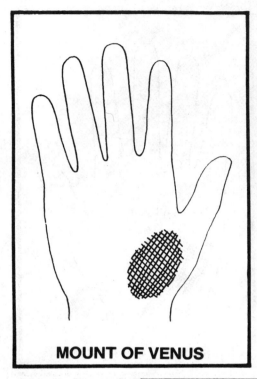

**MOUNT OF VENUS**

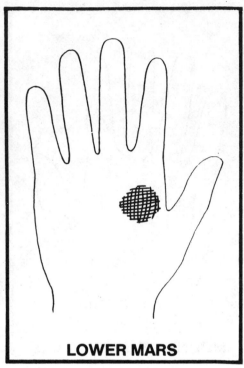

**LOWER MARS**

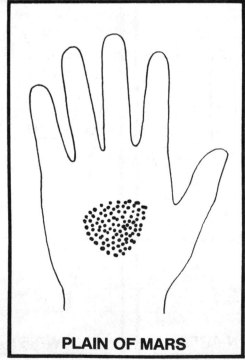

**PLAIN OF MARS**

# MARKS and SIGNS

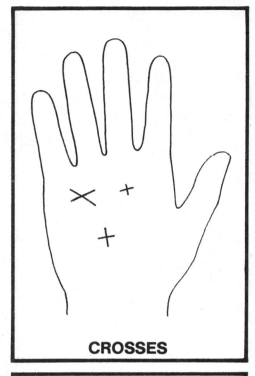

**CROSSES**

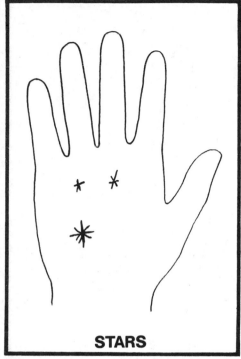

**STARS**

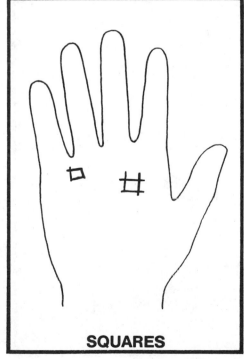

**SQUARES**

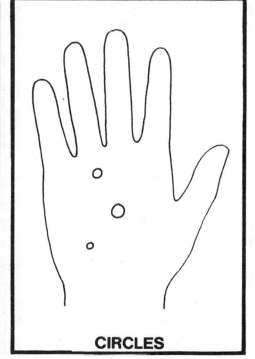

**CIRCLES**

# MARKS AND SIGNS

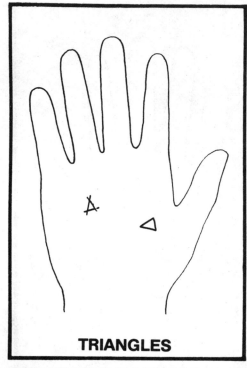

**TRIANGLES**

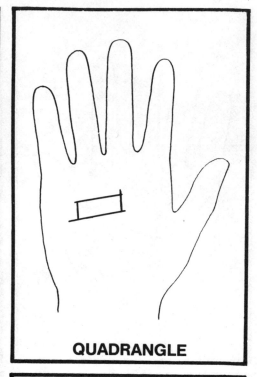

**QUADRANGLE**

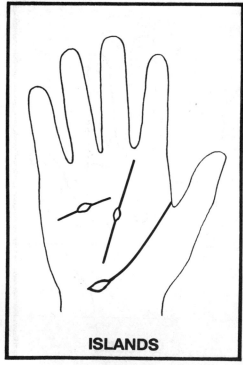

**ISLANDS**

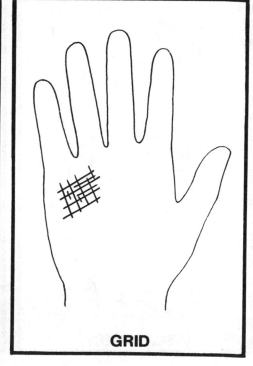

**GRID**

# MARKS and SIGNS

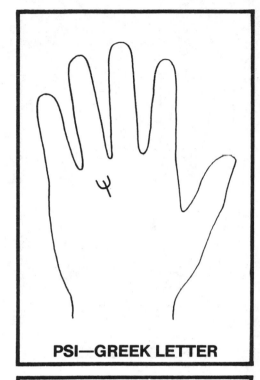

**PSI—GREEK LETTER**

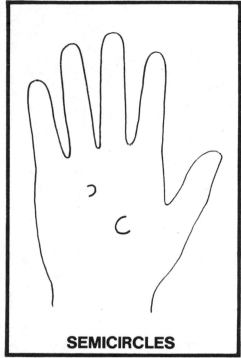

**SEMICIRCLES**

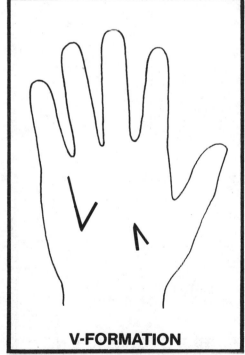

**V-FORMATION**

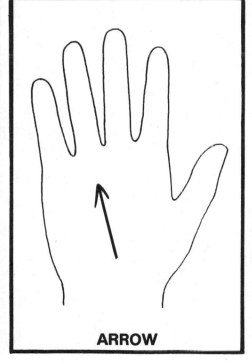

**ARROW**

# MARKS and SIGNS

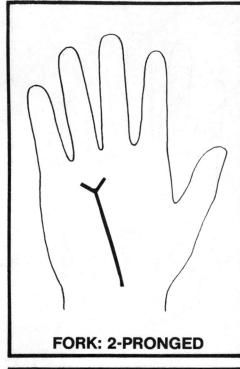

**FORK: 2-PRONGED**

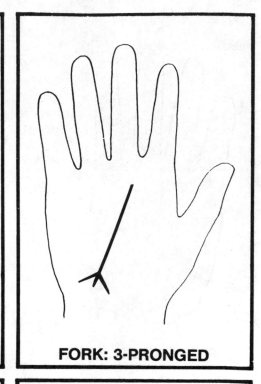

**FORK: 3-PRONGED**

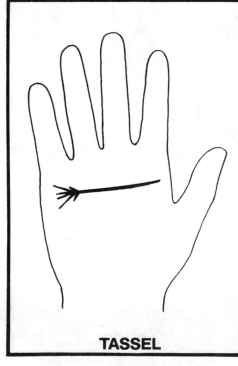

**TASSEL**

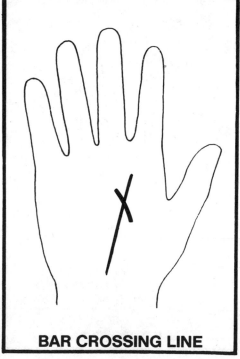

**BAR CROSSING LINE**

# MARKS and SIGNS

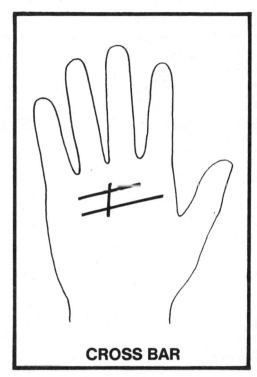

**CROSS BAR**

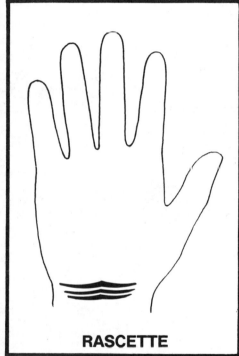

**RASCETTE**

## So You Want To Become A Professional Palmist

The following chapter is a short course in the essentials of professional palmistry. If studied, and through repetition memorized, it should provide you with all the basic elements needed to proceed in a semi-professional manner in the business of palm reading.

A word of caution: I am deeply convinced, in these troubled times, of the need to encourage and comfort clients, rather than reprimand or dominate them. A large number of people who seek out palmists do so as a last resort, after doctors or religious advisers can no longer offer help or relief. In such cases your replies should be palliative, but should also serve to make your client realize he or she still has hidden talents to be utilized—that certain weaknesses can be strengthened, and that he/she still has the potential to serve a unique and useful role in society. Always boost, never knock or criticize.

Everybody wants their palm read. Don't be a fool and do it for nothing. If you go through the trouble to memorize the following text (and it may take you weeks), you deserve a monetary reward. Since it is a mentally draining experience for the palmist, you shouldn't feel bad about asking for due compensation.

How much should you charge? Ask the prospective client, "How much is it worth to you to have your personality and character analyzed and the good news about your future predicted?" I use a sliding scale from $5.00 to $50.00. As you progress, you will, when holding your client's hand, also get messages about this person—either visual or mental. This is the draining part. Some clients are so demanding and ask so many questions that in no time flat you are sapped of all your vitality. Here it is best to start off and say, "Here's a slip of paper. Write down your three questions." If they insist on asking you more questions and interrupt frequently, be bold and tell them you have to charge for every question. With some clients, you will need a day or two to recuperate and rejuvenate your lost cosmic or psychic energy.

A rule of thumb is to never spend more than a half hour reading a palm. The message loses impact after fifteen minutes, and after a half hour, your client has already forgotten what you told him or her in the beginning.

Men oftentimes are more difficult clients than women. Once they unmask and expose their vulnerabilities they should be handled with special care, as they are very gullible and impressionable, and you could inflict lasting damage to a man's psyche during a reading by frightening him with dire forecasts. For that matter avoid answering questions about death, sickness, and accidents, as this is not the business of a palmist.

To drum up business, whenever the opportunity in the conversation presents itself—at a meeting, after class, on line, with acquaintances etc.—just mention very casually that you read palms. You will see that suddenly hands will appear outstretched in your direction and you will hear a chorus of "read my palm." At that point you hand everybody a card with your name and telephone number and say, "Call me, I'm very booked up, so you'll have to make an appointment." Good luck!

# Essentials of Professional Palm Reading

## Short Course

In the following descriptions of lines, shapes, and forms you will see that all lines have a point of origin, a certain length, and a point where they stop. These lines will be decorated with marks. And each mark has a significant interpretation which needs to be memorized. It is necessary sometimes to tell your client at which time in his or her life an event designated by a mark has taken place. This time range is fairly simple to calculate. Take the length of the line in question and divide it into as many segments as the person is old at the time of the reading. You can use a ball-point pen to mark on your client's hand.

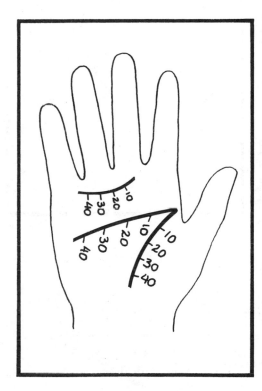
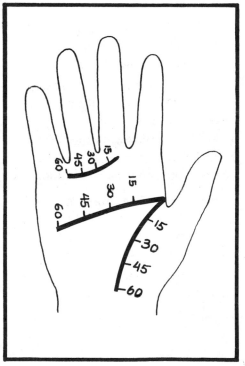

# Life Line

The Life Line is regarded as the most important line on the hand. It starts in the vicinity of the fleshy web of the thumb and runs a curve to a point where the wrist ends. The Life Line is a measure of one's constitution, vitality, willpower, logic, and ability to give and receive love.

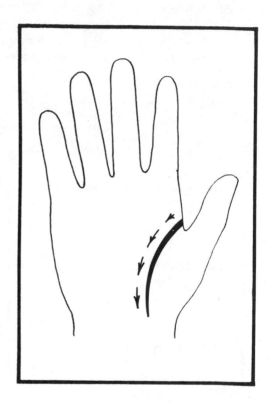

a. If the Life Line encircles the thumb, it is a sign of a long life and activity in old age.

b. If forked at the bottom, it means vital forces escaping from the field of life into the realm of the imagination.

c. Little lines branching down mean one has the tendency to waste vitality.

d. Little lines branching up mean one recuperates quickly.

e. Little lines crossing the Life Line mean one worries too much about unnecessary things.

f. A short and strong Life Line means vitality, drive, and ability to overcome health problems.

g. A Life Line that is straight and close to the thumb depicts a person who lives a careful life spent mostly indoors.

h. Squares on the Life Line give added protection from adverse forces in times of need.

i. A wavy line indicates a person will make many changes in his or her life before coming to inner peace.

# Head Line

The Head Line is the first horizontal line above the Life Line. It starts at a point somewhere between the thumb and the first (Jupiter) finger. This line reveals one's mentality, as expressed by a person's approach to life, attitudes, and career. It is also the measure for potential happiness and success.

a. Joined with the Life Line at the start, it shows a strong sense of mind over body. It belongs to a person with a fearful outlook that is rooted in childhood.

b. Separated at the start from the Life Line, it shows a love of adventure. This person greets life's experiences with enthusiasm.

c. Long, deep, and straight signifies a logical and direct mind with realistic and outstanding intellect.

d. Light and wavy may be interpreted as a lack of ability to concentrate and a lack of depth in thinking, but not a lack of intelligence.

e. A short line implies a tendency towards physical action rather than reflection.

f. A long line slanted upward describes a person with a retentive memory. This is the mark of a collector.

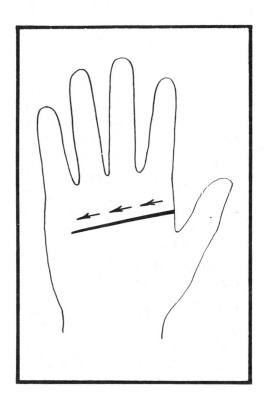

g. A long line swooping down is the mark of the creative, imaginative thinker.

h. A chained line indicates agitations and tensions.

i. A star on the line represents an outstanding mental achievement.

j. A square on the line means guidance from a source outside oneself which lends support in times of need.

k. Forked at the end designates a second childhood.

l. Forked in the middle means an important new interest develops.

# Heart Line

The Heart Line is the first line placed longitudinally at the top of the palm. It runs its course over the mounts across the palm to the edge of the palm (called the Percussion). It expresses the human feelings and handles the affairs and sentiments that are allied to the heart.

a. A chained, broken, or wavy line reveals that its owner is fickle. This person has many love interests, but few of them are stable.

b. A faint line is translated as having a faint heart in romantic affairs.

c. If linked to the ring finger (Apollo) it signifies that marriage might be an impulsive act and may not elevate one's position in life.

d. A star at the start means marital happiness.

e. An island warns of a period of depression.

f. Crosses and breaks indicate emotional losses, or the ending of a love affair.

g. Little lines moving upward mean happiness in love.

h. Little lines descending downward mean disappointments in love.

i. A double line means added protection through someone who loves you.

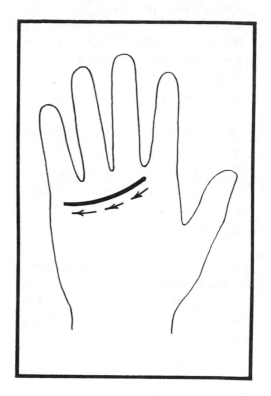

## Saturn Line

The Saturn Line, if perfectly formed, which it seldom is, begins on the palm wrist border (Rascette) and runs vertically across the palm, stopping beneath the second finger (Saturn Finger). This line is the bearer of important psychological manifestations of character, showing strengths and weaknesses as associated with career, friendship, and life's daily problems.

a. A straight, clear line means security and stability in a fixed station in life.

b. Joined to the Life Line at the start signifies a self-made individual, who rises to importance and fame unassisted.

c. Joined to the Life Line at any other point, then separating, means that this person will be called upon to surrender his or her own interests for a time for the sake of others.

d. When it intersects the Life Line from inside the thumb (origin Mount of Venus), it means that members of the family or friends will be helpful in supporting career plans.

e. Origin on the Mount of the Moon places one's destiny in a life under public scrutiny. It designates a rise from obscurity to such fields as entertainment or politics.

f. Influence Lines from the Mount of the Moon that adjoin the Saturn Line mean that romantic interests alter one's destiny. Marriage or an affair will place one in the public eye.

g. If the Saturn Line shifts while crossing the Head Line, this person will manage a successful career change in mid-life.

h. If the Saturn Line rises to the ring finger (Apollo Finger), one's destiny will be profoundly changed by the arts.

i. A star marking the end of the line designates success only after years of hard work.

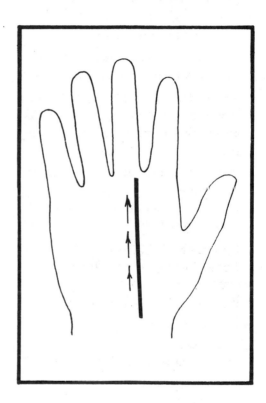

# Apollo Line

The Apollo Line may be found situated anywhere on a straight vertical axis between the wrist and the base of the third finger (Apollo Finger). This line tells about a person's innate potential for success, distinction, and fame through development of special talents. It also tells of rewards gained by solo efforts.

a. If present at all, it implies some degree of public life. A person bearing an Apollo Line at all cannot live in total obscurity.

b. A strong, thick, clearly marked line indicates distinction and self-satisfaction from one's life work.

c. A broken line represents some ups and downs in public acknowledgement.

d. If the Apollo Line ends in a square formation directly beneath the ring finger, it indicates that a kindly patron will help the bearer of this line to achieve high success.

e. Ending in a star, this line reveals spectacular success in the humanities as a writer, musician, painter, or showperson.

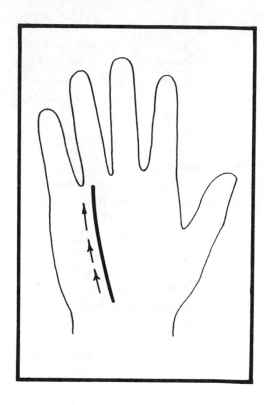

## Mercury Line

The Mercury Line might not always be present. If found, it begins on the heel of the hand near the Rascette and/or the Life Line, and in extreme cases it can extend to the Mount of Mercury beneath the fourth finger (Mercury Finger). Its mere presence alone reveals that its owner is health-oriented and takes measures to retain consistent well-being. A missing line denotes that there are no health problems at all.

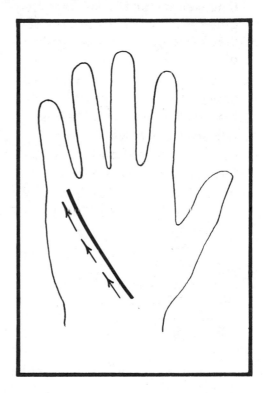

a. A strong, straight line denotes a good sense of business and endless vitality in all moneymaking matters.

b. A wavy line signifies nervous tension.

c. A square on the line indicates protection afforded through medical treatment and/or help in a business crisis.

d. A double line increases the prospect of success in new business ventures. It also promotes marvelous accomplishments and an academically gifted nature.

e. An islanded formation at the start indicates this person will be boosted into a career that will evoke envy.

## Travel Line

The Travel Line begins at the edge of the palm near the heel of the hand, travels across the Mount of the Moon, and traverses the palm horizontally towards the thumb entering the Mount of Venus. Travel Lines mark major overseas or cross-country travels that have a profound effect upon the person's fate.

a. One well-marked Travel Line implies travels, vacations, and relocations of family and job that improve one's lot in life.

b. A Travel Line intersecting the Life Line indicates a trip that will be made for reasons of health. Health improves as a result.

c. A Travel Line criss-crossed by an Interference Line of any kind foretells complications that will arise during travel.

d. Squares on this line supply added protection from danger on the road.

e. Overlaps and breaks are an indication of delays arising during travel.

f. If a Travel Line crosses the Saturn Line, a trip alters one's life for the better.

g. If instead of having one straight Travel Line a person carries several light lines, this designates a jetsetter engaged in frivolous travels without profound influence.

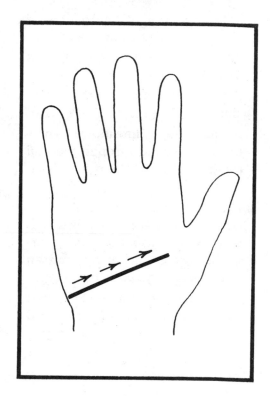

## Money Line

The Money Line can be found starting on the Mount of Venus and ascending upward towards the mounts under the fingers. This line tells of skills at acquiring cash, and recommends the best ways to achieve wealth for the bearer.

a. A line running from the base of the thumb to below the index finger is the mark of a natural money-maker.

b. If the Money Line ends in a star, this is a sign of the "Midas Touch"—everything this person touches turns to riches.

c. If this line points towards the middle finger, it shows that money is best made in business ventures with others.

d. A Money Line cutting across the hand and ending at the fourth finger (Mercury) results in surprise money—won through contests or sweepstakes, found, or acquired through any form of sheer luck.

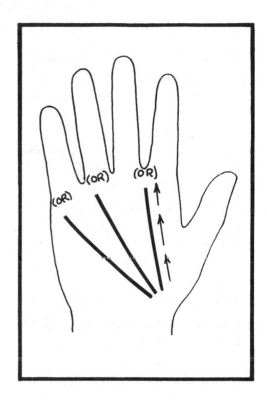

# Marriage Lines

Short horizontal lines that traverse the Mount of Mercury are known as Marriage Lines. In classical palmistry, each Marriage Line is interpreted as a profound emotional tie with a member of the opposite sex that may culminate in marriage. It is usual to find only one Marriage Line per hand.

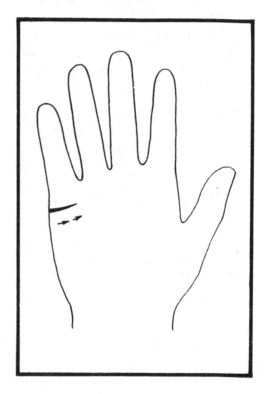

a. The appearance of several Marriage Lines suggests that one may have the potential of forming deep emotional ties with several members of the opposite sex in one lifetime.

b. One clear, deep, long line reveals a happy marriage that lasts a lifetime.

c. A fork at the start of the Marriage Line indicates a long period of engagement.

d. A fork at the end of this line means separation, or termination of a marriage.

e. An overlapping of two lines indicates an affair with another partner while married.

f. A line that breaks, then resumes its course, means that this person will separate from his or her mate and then be reunited.

# ZONES

## PRACTICAL OR IMAGINATIVE

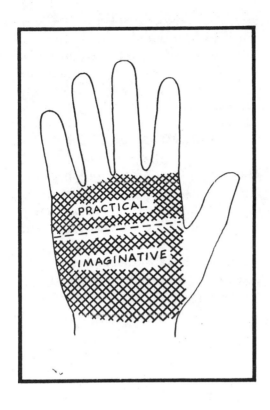

The hand is divided into an upper zone and a lower zone, with the Head Line as the dividing line. All markings on the upper zone denote a person's practical aspects and potentials. Markings on the lower sphere supply information about one's imaginative facilities.

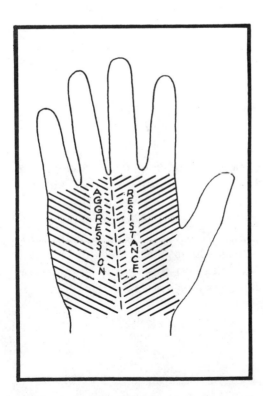

## AGGRESSION OR RESISTANCE

The left side of a person's palm holds those markings that often tell of aggressive behavior. The right side tells of a person's resistive forces and subdued nature. The line of demarcation is usually the Saturn Line.

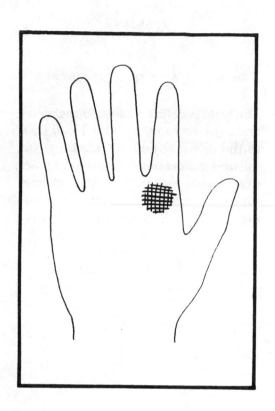

## MOUNTS
### To find the Mounts, have your client cup hand slightly.

## MOUNT OF JUPITER

This mount stands for ambition, pride, honor, and leadership. When well-developed, it shows a love of society and family. Its bearer has pride and self-respect. If excessively large, it manifests conceit. If absent it denotes a lack of self-respect and selfishness. Markings on this mount alter its qualities.

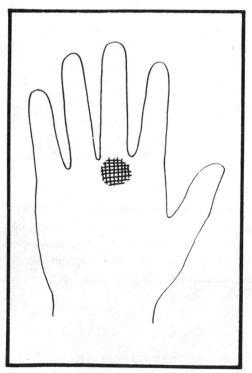

## MOUNT OF SATURN

When well-developed this mount lends to character seriousness and cautious apprehension. If overdeveloped, this person is fretful and worrisome to the point where it interferes with daily activities. Its absence denotes melancholy. Markings on this mount enhance or limit a person's ability to think logically.

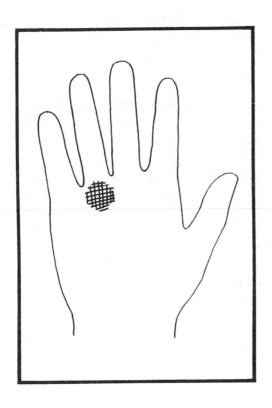

## MOUNT OF APOLLO

A well-padded Mount of Apollo endows a person's character with the qualities of compassion, mercy, love of beauty and art, and a deep desire for recognition and fame. A Mount of Apollo developed to excess denotes vanity and ostentation plus an insatiable desire for money. Its absence denotes cruelty. Markings on this mount influence a person's artistic and emotional propensities.

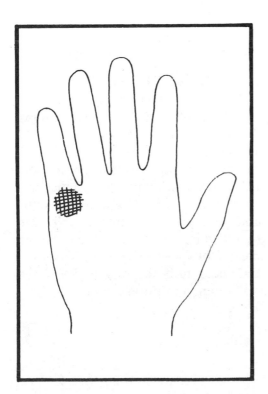

## MOUNT OF MERCURY

A well-developed Mount of Mercury denotes buoyancy, good spiritedness, hopeful attitude, wit, merriment, and enormous recuperative powers. This person can rise swiftly from adversity and learn from difficulties. An excessive Mount of Mercury shows a scheming nature; if missing, it denotes an absence of a sense of humor. Markings on this mount give insight into professional skills and aptitudes.

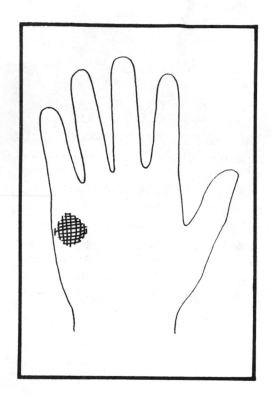

## UPPER MOUNT OF MARS

A large Mount of Mars lends courage, resistance, and a love of danger. A Martian type is an aggressive individual, embodying all the elements of the warrior and having a savage temperament. Markings on this mount describe obstacles encountered and the personality development needed to resist failure and overcome defeat.

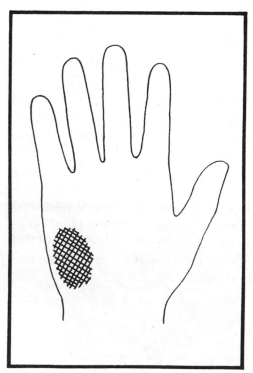

## MOUNT OF THE MOON

A well-developed Mount of the Moon displays imagination and sentimentality. This person loves and needs beautiful surroundings and clothes. This person will travel a lifetime to find just the right setting of harmony, stimulation, and beauty to live and grow in. An overdeveloped Mount of the Moon means folly, caprice, eccentricity, and laziness. If fully absent, it means inner discontent and unrest.

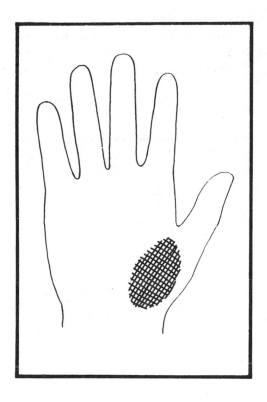

## MOUNT OF VENUS

A good-sized Mount of Venus means a person who is by nature generous, benevolent, affectionate, and inspired by music and the pleasures of the senses. An oversized Mount of Venus denotes unrestricted passions and excessive sensuality, with these forces eventually enslaving its bearer. An absence of this mount denotes a cold and selfish disposition.

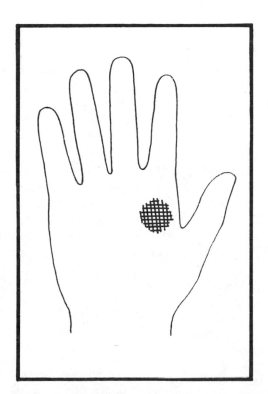

## LOWER MOUNT OF MARS

When well-developed, this mount shows moral courage, extraordinary self-control, and the power to forgive past hurts. If in excess, it signifies reserve and a great strength of resistance. If absent, it shows either little power to withstand the opposition or a weakened endurance. Markings tell of the nature of one's aggressions.

## Star Formations

A Star Formation indicates an event beyond our own free will. It is usually found on the mounts and is a warning signal. It helps to avert danger and threats and is considered a lucky sign.

a. A star on Jupiter means one will win an exalted position in career with little effort.

b. A star on Saturn indicates a dramatic fate, placing its owner in the limelight.

c. A starred Mount of Apollo signifies spectacular success. Recognizing this formation early in life, a person can pick up on his or her strongest talent and quickly become a shooting star of success.

d. A star under Mercury lends distinction in science, medicine, or business.

e. A star on the Mount of the Moon lends imagination and the probability of great mental breakthroughs as a result of creative thinking.

f. A star on Venus is a sure sign of success in anything one touches.

g. A star on Mars protects from agressors and gives one strength to accomplish great things without assistance.

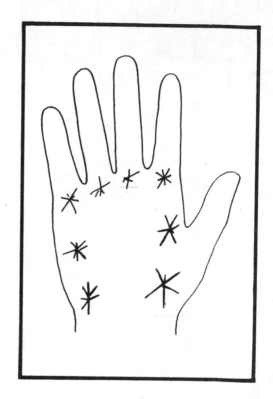

## Squares

A square indicates power. It is formed by the intersection of four minor lines coming from four different directions, which can intersect with or without overlapping at right angles. It tells about opportunities involving common-sense situations that require cool reserve to solve.

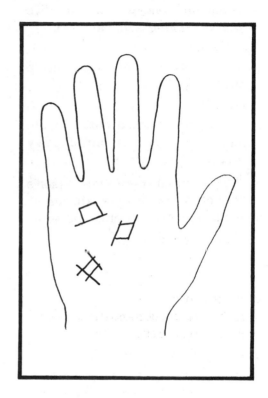

a. A square on Jupiter protects against losses and conflict through opposition of interests.

b. A square on the Mount of Saturn protects an individual from an unkindly fate.

c. A square on the Mount of Mercury supplies added energy and facility in making split-second decisions.

d. A square on the Mount of the Moon protects the traveler from hardships and accidents.

e. A square on the Mount of Mars protects against aggressive and vexatious persons.

# Grid

A grid is a cross-hatching of horizontal and vertical lines, and it may occur anywhere on the palm. It points to problems, but such problems that are open to solving.

a. A grid on Jupiter denotes excessive drive and an overinflated ego.

b. A grid on Apollo means a person who pushes hard for success using all energy reserves.

c. A grid on the Mount of the Moon means this person suffers from imagined fears and is burdened by exaggerated worries.

d. A grid on Mars means this person's anxieties interfere with career achievements and other personal goals.

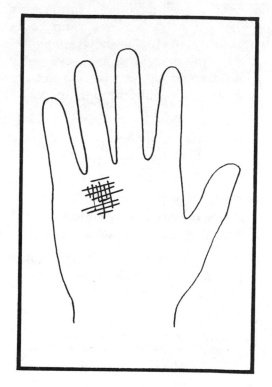

## Triangles

Small triangles are considered fortunate. A triangle improves luck. It is formed by the intersection of three small lines. The sum total of all the angles within the triangle equals 180 degrees.

a. A triangle on Jupiter shows aptitude for diplomacy and a mastery of subtle tactics.

b. A triangle on Saturn means an innate aptitude for the occult.

c. A triangle on the Mount of Apollo announces the discovery of innovative methodology in the arts or sciences.

d. There is a triangle on the Mount of Mercury, which signifies a diplomat, and a person also astute in maneuvering situations to his or her own advantage. This person is evasive and outsmarts even the most clever.

e. A triangle on the Mount of Mars marks excellence in the art of military tactics—a person who thrives on the chill of competition.

f. A triangle on the Mount of the Moon means a highly developed intuitive and imaginative inclination.

g. A triangle on Venus means one is a seeker of material advantages in a love relationship or marital union.

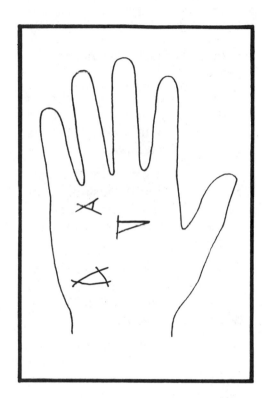

# Crosses

A cross is formed by the intersection of two small, short lines. Crosses define struggles.

a. A cross on Jupiter means a happy union after solving conflicts.

b. A cross on Apollo signifies blunders committed in professional life because of a lack of a balanced approach.

c. A cross on Mercury depicts a shrewd and cunning individual with an inclination to dishonesty, and one who is easily tempted.

d. A cross on Mars shows an obstinate and unbending disposition. This person quarrels frequently and is inclined to lose control and cause bodily harm.

e. A cross on the Mount of the Moon is the mark of a person unable to discern the fine difference between exaggeration and an untruth.

f. A cross on Venus shows a "one and only love." Whether this love be fortunate or unfortunate, a person with this sign will be true to this love till the end.

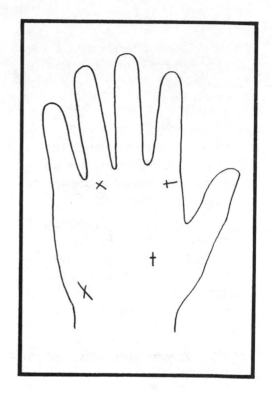

# Bibliography

Achs, Ruth, M.D., and Harper, Rita, M.D. "Diagnostic Palmistry." *Life Magazine*, Feb. 25, 1966, pp. 88-89.

Aria, Gopi. *Palmistry for the New Age.* Long Beach, CA: Morningland Pub. Co., 1977.

Bashir, Mir. *Your Past, Your Present and Your Future through the Art of Hand Analysis.* New York: Doubleday, 1974.

Benham, William G. *The Laws of Scientific Hand Reading.* New York: Hawthorn Books, 1946.

Berry, Theodore J., M.D. *The Hand as a Mirror of Systematic Disease.* Philadelphia: F. A. Davis, 1963.

Berry, Theodore J., M.D. "A Show of Hands." *Time Magazine*, March 13, 1964, p. 84.

Bhat, B.R. *The Indian School of Palmistry.* Coimbatore, 1983.

Bright, J.S. *The Dictionary of Palmistry.* New York: Bell Pub. Co., 1958.

Broekman, Marcel. *The Complete Encyclopedia of Practical Palmistry.* Englewood Cliffs, NJ: Prentice Hall, 1972.

Cavendish, R. "Palmistry." *The Encyclopedia of the Unexplained*, pp. 173-177. New York: McGraw-Hill Book Co., 1976.

Cheiro. *Cheiro's Language of the Hand.* New York: Arco Pub. Co., 1964.

Cheiro, *Cheiro's Palmistry for All.* New York: G. P. Putnam's Sons, 1916.

Cotterman, C.W. "A Scotch-Tape India Ink Method for Recording Dermatoglyphs." *American Journal of Human Genetics*, Vol. 3, p. 376, 1951.

Craig, A.R. *Your Luck's in Your Hand, the Science of Modern Palmistry.* New York: R. Worthington, 1884.

Dale, J.B. *Indian Palmistry.* Theosophical Pub. Co., 1895.

Daniels, Cora L. "Hands, Graphology, Palmistry." *Encyclopedia of Superstitions, Folklore and Occult Sciences of the World*, Vol. 1, pp. 286-294. Detroit: Gale Research Company Book Tower, 1971.

d'Arpetigny, S. *Chirognomie.* Paris, 1843.

Desbarrolles. *Les Mysteres de La Main Reveles et Expliques.* Paris: Librarie du Petit Journal, 1859.

Elbualy, Mussallan S., and Schindler, Joan. *Handbook of Clinical Dermatoglyphs.* Miami: University of Miami Press, 1931.

Frith, Henry. *Palmistry Secrets Revealed.* N. Hollywood, CA: Wilshire Book Co., 1952.

Gettings, Fred. *The Book of the Hand: An Illustrated History of Palmistry.*

London: Paul Hamlyn, 1965.

Gettings, Fred. *The Hand and the Horoscope*. London: Triune Books, 1973.

Gettings, Fred. *Palmistry Made Easy*. London: Bancroft and Co., 1966.

Giles, H.A. "Palmistry in China." *Nineteenth Century*, Vol. LVI, No. 334, pp. 985-988 (1904).

Green, Stephany. *Palmy, Palm Reading Card Game. Teaches Palmistry While You Play*. New York: Merrimack Pub. Co.

Hagen, Johann von. *Chiromantia, Phisiognomia, Astrologia Naturalis*. Strassburg, 1522.

Hastings, James. "Palmistry." *Encyclopedia of Religion and Ethics*. Vol. IX, pp. 591-592. New York: Charles Scribner's Sons, 1955.

Hipskind, Judith. *Palmistry, the Whole View*. St. Paul, MN: Llewellyn Publications, 1977.

Hoffman, Elizabeth P. *Palm Reading Made Easy*. New York: Simon and Schuster, 1971.

Holt, Sarah. *The Genetics of Dermal Ridges*. Springfield, Ill.: Charles C. Thomas, 1968.

Issberner-Haldane, E. *Wissenschaftliche Handlesekunst*. Berlin: Verlag von Karl Siegismund, 1932.

*Life Magazine*. "Diagnostic Palmistry, Simple New Test for Birth Defects." Feb. 25, 1966, pp. 88-89.

MacKenzie, Nancy. *Palmistry for Women*. New York: Warner Paperback, 1973.

*Mademoiselle Magazine*. "Your Fingerprints Might be Clue to a Faulty Heart Valve," p. 24, April, 1977.

Mangoldt, Ursula von. *Der Kosmos in der Hand*. München-Planegg: Otto Wilhelm Barth Verlag, 1934.

Paracelsus, *The Hermetic and Alchemical Writings of Paracelsus*, A.E. Waite, ed. London, 1891.

Price, Derek J. *An Old Palmistry, Being the Earliest Known Book of Palmistry in English* (edited from the Bodelian Ms. Digby Roll IV). Christ's College, Cambridge: W. Heffer and Sons Ltd., 1953. [Original 1440].

Psychos. *The Complete Guide to Palmistry*. New York: Arco Pub. Co., 1971.

Rampa, Lobsang Tuesday. *Feeding the Flame*. Corgi Books, n.d.

Rene, E. *Hands and How to Read Them*. Chicago: Max Stein, 1880.

St. Germain, Comte C. de. *The Practice of Palmistry*. New York: Samuel Weiser, 1897.

St. Hill, Katherine. *The Grammar of Palmistry*. Philadelphia: Henry Altemus, 1893.

Sen, K.C. *Hast Samudrika Shastra, The Science of Hand-Reading Simplified*. Tataporevala Sons and Co., 1951.

Sheridan, Jo. *What Your Hands Reveal*. New York: Bell Publishing, 1958.

Soulie, Charles Georges. *Sciences Occultes en Chine, La Main*. Paris:

Editions Nilsson, 1932.

Spence, Lewis. "Palmistry." *An Encyclopedia of Occultism*, pp. 314-315. New Hyde Park, NY: University Books, 1984.

Spiers, Julian, M.D. *The Hands of Children*. London: Routledge and Kegan, 1955.

Squire, Elizabeth Daniels. *Palmistry Made Practical*. N. Hollywood, CA: Wilshire Book Co., 1976.

Steinbach, Marten. *Medical Palmistry*. New York: Signet, 1975.

Tabori, Paul. *The Book of the Hand, A Compendium of Fact and Legend Since the Dawn of History*. New York: Chilton Book Co., 1962.

Walker, Norma Ford. "Inkless Method of Finger and Palm and Sole Printing." *Journal of Pediatrics*, University of Toronto, Ontario Canada, n.d.

Wilson, Joyce. *The Complete Book of Palmistry*. New York: Bantam, 1971.

Wolff, Charlotte, M.D. *The Hand in Psychological Diagnosis*. New York: Alfred A. Knopf, 1944.

Yi, Ping Koh. *Looking at the Hand*. Hong Kong: Wa Lehn Co., [ca. 1920].

## STAY IN TOUCH. . .
**Llewellyn publishes hundreds of books
on your favorite subjects**

On the following pages you will find listed some books now available on related subjects. Your local bookstore stocks most of these and will stock new Llewellyn titles as they become available. We urge your patronage.

### ORDER BY PHONE

Call toll-free within the U.S. and Canada, **1–800–THE MOON.**

In Minnesota call **(612) 291–1970.**

We accept Visa, MasterCard, and American Express.

### ORDER BY MAIL

Send the full price of your order (MN residents add 7% sales tax) in U.S. funds to :

> **Llewellyn Worldwide,
> P.O Box 64383, Dept. K232-1
> St. Paul, MN 55164–0383, U.S.A.**

### POSTAGE AND HANDLING

- $4.00 for orders $15.00 and under
- $5.00 for orders over $15.00
- No charge for orders over $100.00

We ship UPS in the continental United States. We cannot ship to P.O. boxes. Orders shipped to Alaska, Hawaii, Canada, Mexico, and Puerto Rico will be sent first-class mail.

International orders: Airmail—add freight equal to price of each book to the total price of order, plus $5.00 for each non-book item (audiotapes, etc.).

Surface mail: Add $1.00 per item

Allow 4–6 weeks delivery on all orders. Postage and handling rates subject to change.

### GROUP DISCOUNTS

We offer a 20% quantity discount to group leaders or agents. You must order a minimum of 5 copies of the same book to get our special quantity price.

## Free Catalog

Get a Free copy of our color catalog, *New Worlds of Mind and Spirit*. Subscribe for just $10.00 in the United States and Canada ($20.00 overseas, first-class mail). Many bookstores carry *New Worlds*— ask for it!

## INSTANT HANDWRITING ANALYSIS
### A Key to Personal Success
### Ruth Gardner

For those who wish to increase self-awareness and begin to change some unfavorable aspect of their personality, graphology is a key to success. It can help open our inner selves and explore options for behavior change. With practice, one can make graphology an objective method for giving feedback to the self. And it is an unbeatable channel for monitoring your personal progress.

Author Ruth Gardner makes the process quick and easy, illustrating how letters are broken down vertically into three distinctive zones that help you explore your higher philosophies, daily activities, and primal drives. She also explains how the size, slant, connecting strokes, spacing, and amounts of pressure all say something about the writer. Also included are sections on doodles and social graphology.

*Instant Handwriting Analysis* provides information for anyone interested in pursuing graphology as a hobby or career. It lists many resources for continuing study, including national graphology organizations and several correspondence schools.

0-87542-251-9, 159 pp., 7 x 10, illus., softcover                $15.95


## REVEALING HANDS
### How to Read Palms
### Richard Webster

Palmistry has been an accurate tool for self-knowledge and prediction for thousand of years. The ability to read palms can lead you to a better understanding of yourself, as well as the complex motivations of other people.

Revealing Hands makes it is easier than ever to learn the science of palmistry. As soon as you complete the first chapter, you can begin reading palms with confidence and expertise. Professional palmist and teacher Richard Webster leads you step-by-step through the subject with clear explanations and life-size hand drawings that highlight the points being covered. Whether you are interested in taking up palmistry professionally or just for fun, you will find the information in this book exceptionally entertaining and easy to use.

0-87542-870-3, 304 pp., 7 x 10, 117 illus., softcover                $14.95

## SIGNS OF LOVE
### Your Personal Guide to Romantic and Sexual Compatibility
### Jeraldine Saunders

Unlimited love power can be yours through an intimate knowledge of your horoscope, your numerical birth path, and other vitally important signs and signals that lead the way to loving relationships.

Now in an irresistible approach to the human heart, Jeraldine Saunders, a noted authority on the mystic arts, shows you how to look for love, how to find it, and how to be sure of it. With the aid of astrology, graphology, numerology, palmistry, and face reading, you will discover everything you need to know about your prospects with a given individual. You will learn the two enemies of love and how to eliminate them; the characteristics of all twelve zodiacal signs; the signs that are compatible with yours; the secrets behind your lover's facial features.

*Signs of Love* is the ultimate guide for gaining a better understanding of yourself and others in order to create a meaningful love life and attain lasting happiness.
**0-87542-706-5, 320 pp., 6 x 9, illus., softcover**                       **$6.99**


## THE BOOK OF LOVERS
### Men Who Excite Women, Women Who Excite Men
### Carolyn Reynolds

What are you looking for in a lover or potential mate? If it's money, set your sights on a Pisces/Taurus. Is exercise and health food your passion? Then a Virgo/Cancer will share it with you.

Where do you find these people? They're all here, in *The Book of Lovers.* Astrologer Carolyn Reynolds introduces a new and accurate way to determine romantic compatibility through the use of Sun and Moon sign combinations. And best of all, you don't have to know a single thing about astrology to use this book!

Here you will find descriptions of every man and woman born between the years 1900 and 2000. To see whether that certain someone could be "the one," simply locate his or her birth data in the chart and flip to the relevant pages to read about your person's strengths and weaknesses, sex appeal, personality, and most importantly, how they will treat you!
**0-87542-289-0, 464 pp., 6 x 9, softcover**                         **$14.95**

## PALMISTRY
### The Whole View
### Judith Hipskind

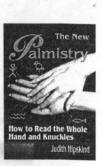

Here is a unique approach to palmistry! Judith Hipskind not only explains how to analyze hands, but also explains why hand analysis works. The approach is based on a practical rationale and is easy to understand. Over 130 illustrations accompany the informal, positive view of hand analysis.

   This new approach to palmistry avoids categorical predictions and presents the meaning of the palm as a synthesis of many factors: the shape, gestures, flexibility, mounts and lives of each hand—as well as a combination of the effects of both heredity and the environment. No part of the hand is treated as a separate unit; the hand reflects the entire personality. An analysis based on the method presented in this book is a rewarding experience for the client—a truly whole view!

**0-87542-306-X, 248 pp., 5¼ x 8, illus., softcover**                    **$9.95**


## THE NEW PALMISTRY
### How to Read the Whole Hand and Knuckles
### Judith Hipskind

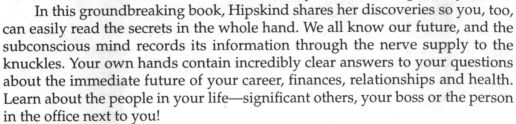

Ten years ago professional palmist Judith Hipskind made a shocking discovery. On the back of a client's hand, and in the knuckles specifically, she saw lines and symbols that revealed as much—if not more—than the palm lines she had studied for some 15 years. Over the next decade, Hipskind researched the knuckles and received verification from hundreds of surprised and satisfied clients on the remarkable accuracy of her amazing new system.

   In this groundbreaking book, Hipskind shares her discoveries so you, too, can easily read the secrets in the whole hand. We all know our future, and the subconscious mind records its information through the nerve supply to the knuckles. Your own hands contain incredibly clear answers to your questions about the immediate future of your career, finances, relationships and health. Learn about the people in your life—significant others, your boss or the person in the office next to you!

**1-56718-352-2, 336 pp., 5¼ x 8, color photos, softcover**                    **12.95**